NEW STUDIES IN BUSINESS WORKBOOK

Junior Certificate Business Studies

MÁIRÉAD ROCHE ■ **DES CUSACK**

Published by
CJ Fallon
Ground Floor – Block B
Liffey Valley Office Campus
Dublin 22
www.cjfallon.ie

First Edition March 2010

Dedication

To David, Conor, Eamonn, David Óg, Margaret, Shane and Aisling.

Contents

Income

Exercises Based on Chapter Content

1 Fill in the blanks in the following sentence.

_____income_____ is money we receive – either _____regular_____ (each week or month) or irregularly (now and again).

2 Tick the correct box (✔) to indicate which of the following are examples of regular or irregular income.

	Regular	Irregular
(a) Social welfare payment	✓	
(b) Gift		✓
(c) Pocket money		✓
(d) Interest	✓	

3 Fill in the blanks in the following statements.

If you are ___employed___ you may receive:

- Salary (monthly)
- ___wages___ (weekly)
- Overtime

- Commission
- Children's allowance
- Company car

- Interest on savings
- Clothing allowance
- Bonus

If you are **unemployed** you may receive:

- ___child___ benefit
- Children's allowance
- Medical ___care___

- Disability benefit
- Family _____ supplement

- Interest on ___Savings___
- Unemployment allowance

A ___Student___ may receive:

- Pocket money
- Gift
- Medical card

- Interest on savings
- Wage (part-time)
- Student grant

An **old age pensioner** may receive:

- Free travel
- _____ (part-time)
- Interest ___on savings___

- Medical card
- Gift
- Pension

4 Use the following blank payslip to answer Question 7 on page 5 of the textbook.

Week No.	Gross Pay			Deductions					Date	Employee No. 429
Name	Basic	Overtime	Total	PAYE	PRSI	Pension	Union	Total Deductions		Net Pay
Sheila Fitz.										

5   Use the following blank payslip to answer Question 8 on page 5 of the textbook.

Week No.	Gross Pay			Deductions				Date	Employee No. 124
Name	Basic	Overtime	Total	PAYE	PRSI	Pension	Union	Total Deductions	Net Pay
eter Ye	132	72	50	53	35	50		64	356

6   Use the following blank payslip to answer Question 9 on page 5 of the textbook.

Week No.	Gross Pay			Deductions				Date	Employee No. 87
Name	Basic	Overtime	Total	PAYE	PRSI	Pension	Union	Total Deductions	Net Pay
E D	58	45	30	10	15	73		50	56

7   Use the following blank payslip to answer Question 10 on page 5 of the textbook.

Week No.	Gross Pay			Deductions				Date	Employee No. 26
Name	Basic	Overtime	Total	PAYE	PRSI	Pension	Union	Total Deductions	Net Pay

8   **(a)** Which of the following are statutory deductions on a wage slip? Tick (✔) the appropriate box in each case.

Trade Union	☐	PAYE	☐	Savings	☐
VHI	☐	Holidays	☐	PRSI	☐

(b) Explain, giving one example, what is meant by a 'benefit in kind'.

_____

_____

9   Use the following blank payslip to answer Question 12(c) on page 5 of the textbook.

Week No.	Gross Pay			Deductions				Date	Employee No. _____
Name	Basic	Overtime	Total	PAYE	PRSI	Pension	Union	Total Deductions	Net Pay

 EXERCISES

1 Calculate the gross and net pay in each of the following cases.
   (a) Pat Higgins earns €350 per week and receives a commission of 12% on sales of €1,000. His PAYE is €65, PRSI is €40, income levy is €20, trade union deduction is €13 and credit union deduction is €30.
   (b) Alex Campbell works 39 hours per week at €14 per hour. He earns double time at weekends. He worked Saturday afternoon for 4 hours. His PAYE deduction is €45, PRSI is €20 and pension levy is €60.
   (c) Wendy Bently works part time at a dog kennels. She earns €12 per hour and worked 24 hours this week. She also earns a bonus of €20 for dog grooming and she groomed five dogs this week. Her PAYE is €45, PRSI is €28, income levy is €30 and savings are €58.
   (d) Michael Philips is an insurance salesman and earns €450 per week. He pays 23% PAYE, 12% PRSI and an income levy of 1%.

2 Prepare a payslip for each person in Question 1 above.
   (a)

Week No.	Gross Pay			Deductions				Date	Employee No. _____
Name	Basic	Overtime	Total	PAYE	PRSI	Pension	Union	Total Deductions	Net Pay
Pat Higgins									

   (b)

Week No.	Gross Pay			Deductions				Date	Employee No. _____
Name	Basic	Overtime	Total	PAYE	PRSI	Pension	Union	Total Deductions	Net Pay
Alex Campbell									

   (c)

Week No.	Gross Pay			Deductions				Date	Employee No. _____
Name	Basic	Overtime	Total	PAYE	PRSI	Pension	Union	Total Deductions	Net Pay
Wendy Bently									

   (d)

Week No.	Gross Pay			Deductions				Date	Employee No. _____
Name	Basic	Overtime	Total	PAYE	PRSI	Pension	Union	Total Deductions	Net Pay
Michael Philips									

Expenditure

Exercises Based on Chapter Content

1 Insert the following items of spending under the correct heading in the grid below.

Rent   Mortgage   Food   Insurance (car, house & life)
Electricity   Gas   Heating (oil/coal)   Telephone
Clothes   Car tax   TV licence   School books
Petrol/travel   Pocket money   Entertainment   Loan repayments
Holidays   Gifts   Decorating   Furniture
School uniforms   Car service   Local charges   Newspapers/magazine
Beauty treatments   Computer and other games   Photography   Phone credit
Chemist

Fixed spending	Irregular spending	Discretionary spending
rent	clothes	holidays
mortgage	petrol	beauty
car tax	electricity	gifts
pocket money	uniforms	computer games
TV licence	chemist	entertainment
insurance	gas	decorating
telephone	car service	photography
school books	food	furniture
loan repayment	heating	newspaper
	phone credit	

2 Draft the budgeted spending for Anna James for the next 4 weeks.
Rent: €55 weekly. Loan repayment: €20 weekly.
Food: week 1 = €40; week 2 = €48; week 3 = €37; week 4 = €45.
Travel: week 1 = €15; week 2 = €20; week 3 = €15; week 4 = €22.
Spending on clothes: week 2 = €80.
Entertainment: week 1 = €40; week 2 = €35; week 3 = €30 and rising by €5 for week 4.
Magazines: €6 usually and €7.50 in week 3. Lotto: €2 per week.

	Week 1	Week 2	Week 3	Week 4	Total
Expenditure	€	€	€	€	€
Fixed					
Rent	55	55	55	55	220
Loan repayment	20	20	20	20	80
Subtotal	75	75	75	75	300
Irregular					
Food	40	48	37	45	170
Travel	15	20	15	22	72
Clothes	—	80	—	—	80
Subtotal	65	148	52	67	332
Discretionary					
Entertainment	40	35	30	35	140
Magazines	6	6	7.50	6	25.5
Lotto	2	2	2	2	8
Subtotal	48	43	39.50	43	173.50
Total	178	266	166.50	185	~~810~~ 795.5

3 Tick the correct box (✔) to indicate whether each of the following are examples of current or capital expenditure.

		Current spending	Capital spending
(a)	Purchase of a car €13,000		✔
(b)	Ice cream €1.59	✔	
(c)	Petrol for car €45	✔	
(d)	Digital camera €199		✔
(e)	Service of car €99	✔	
(f)	Ink for printer €45	✔	
(g)	Trees for garden €55		✔
(h)	Birthday cake €7	✔	

4 Calculate the number of units used in each of the following meter readings.

Date	Present	Previous	Units used
Oct–Nov 2011	1,122	900	
Dec 2011–Jan 2012	1,322	1,122	
Feb–March 2012	1,567	1,322	
April–May 2012	1,879	1,567	
June–July 2012	2,012	1,879	

5 Electricity costs €0.21 per unit. Calculate the cost of electricity used for each of the periods in Question 4 above.

Date	Units used	Cost €
Oct–Nov 2011		
Dec 2011–Jan 2012		
Feb–March 2012		
April–May 2012		
June–July 2012		

6 Fill in the following grids using the information given in Question 11 on page 15 of the textbook.

(a)

Donegan	Jan	Feb	March	April	May	June	Total
	€	€	€	€	€	€	€
Fixed							
Mortgage	125						
Car payment							
Total							
Irregular							
Electricity							
Fuel							
Household expenses							
Discretionary							
Films							
Video rental							
Total							

(b)

O'Connell	Jan	Feb	March	April	May	June	Total
	€	€	€	€	€	€	€
Fixed							
Mortgage							
Term loan repayment							
Car payment							
TV loan							
Subtotal							
Irregular							
Food							
Electricity							
Bus fares							
Dance classes							
Music lessons							
School books							
TV licence							
Dog licence							
Subtotal							
Discretionary							
Rugby match							
Wedding present							
Subtotal							
Total expenditure							

Budgeting

Exercises Based on Chapter Content

This chapter combines income and expenditure and nets the two to find the actual cash position at the end of each week/month. Remember that the closing cash of one month is the opening cash of the next. Opening cash in the first month is the opening cash in total.

1 Complete the following budgets (last 3 lines).

(a)

	Feb	March	April	May	Total
	€	€	€	€	€
Total income A	1,970	1,970	1,990	2,060	7,990
Total expenditure B	1,750	1,815	1,725	3,385	8,675
Net cash A-B	220	155	265	-1325	-685
Opening cash	2,000	2200	2355	2620	2000
Closing cash	2200	2355	2620	1295	1315

(b)

	Feb	March	April	May	Total
	€	€	€	€	€
Total income A	2,970	5,970	2,990	2,060	13990
Total expenditure B	3,750	2,815	1,325	3,985	11255
Net cash A-B	(780)	3155	1665	(1925)	2745
Opening cash	4,000	3220	6375	8040	4000
Closing cash	3220	6375	8040	6115	

(c)

	Feb	March	April	May	Total
	€	€	€	€	€
Total Income	3,060	3,060	3,060	3,060	12,240
Total expenditure	3,820	2,240	2,820	1,620	10,500
Net cash	(760)	820	240	1440	1740
Opening cash	100	660	1480	1720	100
Closing cash	660	1480	1720	1840	1840

(d)

	Feb	March	April	May	Total
	€	€	€	€	€
Total Income	2,100	2,900	4,500	1,200	
Total expenditure	3,820	2,240	2,820	1,620	
Net cash					
Opening cash	600				
Closing cash					

(e)

	Jan	Feb	March	Total
	€	€	€	€
Income	5,633	5,988	5,332	
Total expenditure	3,820	3,390	4,820	
Net cash				
Opening cash	750			
Closing cash				

Blank Documents for Answering Questions 1–7 on pages 20–26 of the Textbook

2 Complete the following budget by filling in the net cash opening cash and closing cash columns.

Planned Income	Feb	March	April	May	Total
	€	€	€	€	€
Gabriel Kent	1,200	1,200	1,200	1,270	4,870
June Avalon	670	670	690	690	2,720
Child benefit	100	100	100	100	400
Total income	**1,970**	**1,970**	**1,990**	**2,060**	**7,990**
Planned expenditure					
Fixed					
Mortgage	600	600	600	600	2,400
Apartment (house) insurance	80	80	80	80	320
Car insurance	45	45	45	45	180
Subtotal	**725**	**725**	**725**	**725**	**2,900**
Irregular					
Car running costs	270	240	230	280	1,020
Light and heat	130	110	100	80	420
Household expenses	450	400	370	400	1,620
Subtotal	**850**	**750**	**700**	**760**	**3,060**
Discretionary					
Holiday				1,800	1,800
Entertainment	300	340	300	100	1,040
Subtotal	**300**	**340**	**300**	**1,900**	**2,840**
Total expenditure	**1,875**	**1,815**	**1,725**	**3,385**	**8,800**
Net cash	95	155	265	(1325)	(810)
Opening cash	2,000	1905	2060	2325	2000
Closing cash	1905	2060	2325	–1000	1190

3 Complete the following household budget for the O'Regan family.

Planned Income	Feb	March	April	May	Total
	€	€	€	€	€
Unemployment benefit	950	950	950	950	3,800
Child allowance	500	500	500	500	2,000
Total income	**1,450**	**1,450**	**1,450**	**1,450**	**5,800**
Planned expenditure					
Fixed					
Rent	400	400	400	400	1,600
Insurance	60	60	60	60	240
Subtotal	**460**	**460**	**460**	**460**	**1,840**
Irregular					
Electricity	125	114	104	90	433
Household expenses	560	670	543	669	2,442
Subtotal	**685**	**784**	**647**	**759**	**2,875**
Discretionary					
Entertainment	200	150	170	200	720
Concert tickets			250		250
Subtotal	**200**	**150**	**420**	**200**	**970**
Total expenditure					
Net cash					
Opening cash	500				
Closing cash					

4 Complete the following adjusted budget for the O'Regan family.

Planned Income	Feb	March	April	May	Total
	€	€	€	€	€
Unemployment benefit	950	950	950	950	3,800
Child allowance	400	400	400	400	
Total income					
Planned expenditure					
Fixed					
Rent	400	400	400	400	1,600
Insurance	60	60	60	60	240
Subtotal					
Irregular					
Electricity	125	114	104	90	433
Household expenses	340	440	393	400	
Subtotal					
Discretionary					
Entertainment	100	50	70	100	
Concert tickets			100		
Subtotal					
Total expenditure					
Net cash					
Opening cash	500				
Closing cash					

5 Complete the following household budget for the Baker family.

Planned Income	Feb	March	April	May	Total
	€	€	€	€	€
Unemployment benefit	300	300	300	350	
Child allowance	90	90	90	90	
Total income			390	440	
Planned expenditure					
Fixed					
Rent	90	90	90	90	
Insurance	46	46	46	46	
Subtotal	136	136	136	136	544
Irregular					
Electricity	121		103		
Household expenses	355	369	344	399	
Subtotal	476	369	447	399	
Discretionary					
Entertainment	60	80	75	70	
Rugby match		70			
Subtotal	60	150	75	70	
Total expenditure	672	655			
Net cash	-282	-265	-268	-65	-880
Opening cash	400	118	-147		
Closing cash	118	-147	-415		

6 Complete the following household budget for the Bishop family.

Planned Income	Jan	Feb	March	April	Total Jan-April	Estimate May-Dec	Total for the year
	€	€	€	€	€	€	€
Salaries							
Joan	1,600	1,600	1,600	1,600	6,400	12,800	19,200
Peter	1,400	1,400	1,400	1,400	5,600	11,200	16,800
Child benefit	60	60	60	60	240	480	720
Total income	**3,060**	**3,060**	**3,060**	**3,060**	**12,240**	**24,480**	**36,720**
Expenditure							
Fixed							
Mortgage	700	700	700	700	2,800	5,600	8,400
Annual tax on car	480				480		480
Car loan	560	560	560		1,680		1,680
Annual car insurance	800				800		800
House insurance	40	40	40	40	160	320	480
Subtotal	**2,580**	**1,300**	**1,300**	**740**	**5,920**	**5,920**	**11,840**
Irregular							
Household costs	600	600	600	600	2,400	4,800	7,200
Car running costs	140	140	320	140	740	1,360	2,100
Electricity	400		500		900	1,440	2,340
Subtotal	**1,140**	**740**	**1,420**	**740**	**4,040**	**7,600**	**11,640**
Discretionary							
Birthdays		100		40	140	140	280
Entertainment	100	100	100	100	400	3,600	4,000
Subtotal	**100**	**200**	**100**	**140**	**540**	**3,740**	**4,280**
Total expenditure	**3,820**	**2,240**	**2,820**	**1,620**	**10,500**	**17,260**	**27,760**
Net cash	−760	820	240	1440	1740	7220	8960
Opening cash	100	−660	160	380	1820	3560	100
Closing cash	−660	140	380	1820	3560	10780	9060

7 Draft the planned budget for Gabriel Kent and June Avalon for the four months from February to May.
- They have opening cash of €2,000.
- Gabriel has a monthly income of €1,200 and he expects a bonus of €70 in May.
- June works part-time and had a changeable hour's income in February and March of €670 and bonus of €20 in April and May.
- They receive child benefit of €100 monthly.
- They have to pay a mortgage of €600.
- The insurance on the flat is €960 per year, payable monthly.
- Insurance on the family car is €540 per year, payable monthly.
- The car costs €270 to run in February, €40 in March, €230 in April and €280 in May.
- Light and heat for February is €130. It drops by €20 in March, €100 in April and €80 in May.
- Household running costs/expenses are €450 in February, €370 in April and €400 in March and May.
- They plan to holiday in Spain in May, cost €1,800.
- Entertainment is usually €300, rising by €40 in April and dropping to €100 in May.

Planned Income	Jan	Feb	March	April	Total Jan-April
	€	€	€	€	€
Gabriel Kent	1200	1200	1200	1200	4800
June Avalon		670	670	20	1360
Child benefit	100	100	100	100	400
Total income	1300	1970	1970	1320	6560
Planned expenditure					
Fixed					
Mortgage	450	450	450	450	2800
Flat (house) insurance	80	80	80	80	320
Car insurance	45	45	45	45	180
Subtotal	175	175	175	175	700
Irregular					
Car running costs		270	40	230	540
Light and heat		130	110	100	340
Household expenses		450	400	370	1220
Subtotal		850	550	700	2100
Discretionary					
Holiday					
Entertainment	300	300	300	340	880
Subtotal	300	300	300	200	880
Total expenditure	475	1325	1025	1075	3680
Net cash	825	645	945	245	2960
Opening cash	2000	2825	3470	4415	2000
Closing cash	2825	3470	4415	4660	4960

8 Here is the estimated budget for the McCarthy family.

Planned Income	Jan	Feb	March	April	Total Jan-April	Estimate May-Dec	Total for the year
	€	€	€	€	€	€	€
Salaries							
Joan	1,600	1,600	1,600	1,600	6,400	13440	19840
Peter	1,400	1,400	1,400	1,400	5,600	12320	17920
Child benefit	60	60	60	60	240	480	720
Total income	**3,060**	**3,060**	**3,060**	**3,060**	**12,240**	26240	38480
Expenditure							
Fixed							
Mortgage	700	700	700	700	2,800	5180	7980
Annual tax on car	480				480	–	480
Car loan	560	560	560		1,680	–	1680
Annual car insurance	800				800	–	800
House insurance	40	40	40	40	160	320	480
Subtotal	**2,580**	**1,300**	**1,300**	**740**	**5,920**	5500	11420
Irregular							
Household costs	600	600	600	600	2,400	4800	7200
Car running costs	140	140	320	140	740	1360	2100
Electricity	400		500		900	1440	2340
Subtotal	**1,140**	**740**	**1,420**	**740**	**4,040**	7600	11640
Discretionary							
Birthdays		100		40	140	140	280
Entertainment	100	100	100	100	400	3600	4000
Subtotal	**100**	**200**	**100**	**140**	**540**	3740	4280
Total expenditure	**3,820**	**2,240**	**2,820**	**1,620**	**10,500**	16840	27340
Net cash	-760	820	240	1,440	1,740	9400	11140
Opening cash	100	-660	160	400	100	1840	100
Closing cash	-660	160	400	1,840	920	11240	11240

The McCarthys use the following information to draft their estimated budget.

- Joan is due a salary increase of 5% from 1 May.
- Peter will get a salary increase of 10% from 1 September.
- Child benefit income will continue as for first four months of year.
- The mortgage will be reduced by €140 per month from 1 October.
- House insurance per month will continue as for the first four months of the year.
- Household costs per month should stay the same as for the first four months of the year.
- Car running costs will cost €140 per month until the end of the year. New tyres will be needed in September costing €240.
- The total cost of the electricity charges for the whole of 2011 is expected to be €2,340.
- Birthdays will cost another €140 before the end of 2011.
- Entertainment is expected to cost a total of €1,000 for the whole year.
- The McCarthys are going on a holiday to Greece in August costing €3,000.

9 Complete the budget for the Maolain family using the information given in Question 8 on page 27 of the textbook.

Maolain family	May	June	July	August	Total
	€	€	€	€	€
Planned Income					
Total					
Expenditure					
Fixed					
Subtotal					
Irregular					
Subtotal					
Discretionary					
Subtotal					
Total expenditure					
Net cash					
Opening cash					
Closing cash					

10 Complete the budget for the Aodh family using the information given in Question 9 on page 27 of the textbook.

Aodh family	Jan	Feb	March	April	Total
	€	€	€	€	€
Planned income					
Hugh Aodh					
Katelyn Aodh					
Total					
Expenditure					
Fixed					
Subtotal					
Irregular					
Subtotal					
Discretionary					
Subtotal					
Total expenditure					
Net cash					
Opening cash					
Closing cash					

11 Complete the budget for the Guirey family using the information given in Question 10 on page 28 of the textbook.

	Jan	Feb	March	April	Total
	€	€	€	€	€
Planned income					
Michael Guirey					
Caroline Guirey					
Child benefit					
Total					
Expenditure					
Fixed					
Subtotal					
Irregular					
Subtotal					
Discretionary					
Subtotal					
Total expenditure					
Net cash					
Opening cash					
Closing cash					

12 Complete the budget for the Best family using the information given in Question 11 on page 28 of the textbook.

(a)

Best family	Sept	Oct	Nov	Dec	Total
	€	€	€	€	€
Planned income					
Total					
Expenditure					
Fixed					
Subtotal					
Irregular					
Subtotal					
Discretionary					
Subtotal					
Total expenditure					
Net cash					
Opening cash					
Closing cash					

(b) Name one other means by which the Best family could pay an electricity bill.

_____

(c) Tick the correct box.
   Prize bonds are:
   fixed expenditure ☐
   irregular expenditure ☐
   discretionary expenditure ☐

13 The Walsh family prepare a detailed budget for a few months and then estimate spending and income for the rest of the year. In this way, they can find total planned income and spending for the year. Here is a detailed planned budget for the Walsh household for four months (Jan to April). (Question 12 on page 29 of the textbook.)

Income	Jan	Feb	March	April	Total Jan-April	Estimate May-Dec	Total for the year
	€	€	€	€	€	€	€
Salaries							
Tim	500	500	500	500	2000	14 280	16280
Eilin	900	900	900	900	3600	39 660	43200
Child benefit	300	300	300	300	1200	2100	3300
Total income	1700	1700	1700	1700	6800	55980	62780
Expenditure							
Fixed							
Mortgage	900	900	900	900	3600	6780	10380
Annual tax on car			600		600	—	600
Car loan	350	350	350	350	1400	—	1400
Annual car insurance			870		870	—	870
House insurance	60	60	60	60	240	480	720
Subtotal	1310	1310	2780	1310	6710	7260	13970
Irregular							
Household costs	699	766	500	698	2663		
Car running costs	250	230	199	240	919	1120	~~2039~~ 2279
Electricity	177		145		322	585	907
Subtotal	1126	996	844	938	3904	1705	3186
Discretionary							
Birthdays	120			80	200	300	500
Entertainment	140	150	155	130	575	3925	4500
Subtotal	260	150	155	210	775	4225	5000
Total expenditure	2696	2456	3779	2458	11389	13190	22156
Net cash	−996	−756	−2079	−758	−4589	42790	40624
Opening cash	2,000	1004	248	−1831	−2589	−7178	2000
Closing cash	1004	248	−1831	−2589	−7178	35612	42624

The Walsh family uses the following information to draft their estimated budget.
- Tim is due a salary increase of 5% from 1 May.
- Eilin will get a salary increase of 10% from 1 September.
- Child benefit income will decrease by €100 in October.
- The mortgage will be reduced by €140 per month from 1 October.
- House insurance per month will continue as for the first four months of the year.
- Household costs per month should stay the same as the first four months of the year.
- Car running costs will be €140 per month until the end of the year. New tyres will be needed in September costing €240.
- The total cost of the electricity charges for the whole of 2011 is expected to be €2,340 (paid every second month).
- Birthdays will cost another €300 before the end of 2011.
- Entertainment is expected to cost a total of €1,500 for the whole year.
- The Walsh family are going on a holiday to Euro Disney in July costing €3,000.

14 Complete the revised budget for the Stackpoole family using the information given in Question 13 on page 30 of the textbook.

	Original Budget				Revised Budget			
	July	Aug	Sept	Total	July	Aug	Sept	Total
Planned Income	€	€	€	€	€	€	€	€
Mr Stackpoole	3,000	3,000	3,000	9,000				
Mrs Stackpoole	2,240	2,240	2,240	6,720				
Child benefit	320	320	320	960				
Total income	5,560	5,560	5,560	16,680				
Planned expenditure								
Fixed								
Mortgage	1,600	1,600	1,600	4,800				
Loan repayments	800	800	800	2,400				
Car insurance	70	70	70	210				
Subtotal	2,470	2,470	2,470	7,410				
Irregular								
Household costs	1,500	1,500	1,500	4,500				
Car costs	300	300	300	900				
Light and heat	490		380	870				
Telephone costs	100	100	280	480				
Subtotal	2,390	1,900	2,460	6,750				
Discretionary								
Entertainment costs	400	400	400	1,200				
Presents	600		500	1,100				
Holiday			10,000	10,000				
Subtotal	1,000	400	10,900	12,300				
Total expenditure	5,860	4,770	15,830	26,460				
Net cash	-300	790	-10,270	-9,780				
Opening cash	1,000	700	1,490	1,000				
Closing cash	700	1,490	8,780	8,780				

Household Accounts

1   Name the three record books used in Junior Certificate Business Studies.

(a) _Record book 1_   (b) _Record book 2_   (c) _Record book 3._

2   Balance the following account.

Date	Details	F	Total €	Date	Details	F	Total €
5/2/11	Wages		550	6/2/11	Rent		156
				8/3/11	Lotto tickets		6
				10/2/11	Clothes		100
					Balance c/d		288
			550				550
	Balance b/d		288				

3   Fill in the gaps in the following sentences (don't forget to memorise this!).

How to balance an account

1. Add both sides (on a rough piece of paper).

2. Take the _____ Small Side _____ from the big side (on a rough piece of paper).

3. Name the answer as the _____ Balance c/d _____.

4. Add the balance to the _____ Smaller Side _____ side in the account.

5. Now total both sides again _____ in the _____ account.

6. Draw a single line above and a _____ double _____ red line under the total

   (these totals should be the same and on the _____ same _____ line).

7. Bring the balance down to the opposite side (_____ Bigger _____ side).

4   Balance the following account.

Date	Details	Total €	Date	Details	Total €	Groceries €	Light & heat €	Shoes & clothes €	Car €	Other €
1 April	Balance	820	2 April	Shoes	70			70		
			4	Groceries	186	186				
4	Child benefit	100	6	Electricity	87		87			
25	Wages	1,320	8	Petrol	52				52	
28	Old furniture sale	250	11	Heat oil	200		200			
			15	Car repair	130				130	
			19	Clothes	146			146		
			25	Groceries	234	234				
			26	Hospital	800					800
				Balance c/d	585					
						420	287	216	182	800
	Balance b/d	585								

5 Examine the following budget comparison statement for the Dowen Family and fill in the missing figures.

	Budget	Actual	Difference
Wages	1,300	1,320	+ 20
Child benefit	100		−
Other income	−	250	+ 250
Total income	**1,400**	**1,670**	**+ 270**
Expenditure			
Groceries	400	420	+ 20
Light and heat	270	287	+ 17
Shoes and clothes		216	− 4
Car	170	182	+ 12
Other	−	800	
Total expenditure	**1,060**	**2,612**	**+1,552**
Net cash	340		− 1,282
	Prepared on 1 April	Prepared on 31 April approx	

The Dowens overspent on groceries, _Light and heat_____ car and other and they

underspent on _____Shoes and clothes._____ and clothes.

6 Balance the following account and total the analysis columns.

Date 2013	Details	F	Cash	Bank	Date 2013	Details	Cheque no.	Cash	Bank	Grocery	Travel	Rent	Other
2 Oct	Wages		224	440	2 Oct	Rent	24		120			120	
						Grocery	25		129.90	129.90			
						Travel		7			7		
					3 Oct	Travel		7			7		
						Clothes	26		51.96				51.96
					4 Oct	Travel		6			6		
						Grocery		11		11			
					5 Oct	Travel		6			6		
						Grocery		12.80		12.80			
					7 Oct	Hair	27		40				40
						Entertainment		46					46
					8 Oct	Donation		4					4
						Entertainment		32					32
						Balance c/d		92.20	98.14				
			224	440				224	440				
	Balance b/d		92.20	98.14									

7 Complete the following analysed cash book for the Hope family using the details provided in Question 15 on page 40 of the textbook.

Date	Details	Bank	Date	Details	Bank	Food	Light & heat	Car	Entertainment	Other
June 2	Wages	780	June 4	Groceries	170	170				
June 6	C.Benefit	110	June 4	Petrol	45			45		
			June 6	Clothes	156					156
			June 7	bus ticket	45					45
			June 7	T.V.	157					157
			June 9	Groceries	230	230				
			June 9	Car Service	230			230		
			June 9	NCT	50			50		
			June 11	Cinema	60				60	
			June 11	Meal out	80	80				
				Balance c/d	333					
		1223			1223					
	Balance b/d	333								

8 Complete the following analysed cash book for the O'Connor family using the details provided in Question 16 on page 41 of the textbook. 1720

Date	Details	Bank	Date	Details	Bank	Food	Clothes	Entertainment	Other
Apr 1	Balance	350	Apr 5	Petrol	55				55
Apr 7	Salary	970	Apr 8	Meat	159	159			
Apr 14	Salary	400	Apr 9	Groceries	265	265			
			Apr 11	Electricity	187				187
			Apr 12	Car	160				160
			Apr 13	LawnMower	95				95
			Apr 15	Groceries	267	267			
			Apr 16	Dinner	156			156	
				Balance c/d	376				
		1720			1720				
	Balance b/d	376							

9 Complete the following analysed cash book for the Hartnett family using the details provided in Question 17 on page 41 of the textbook.

Date	Details	Bank	Date	Details	Bank	Food	Clothes	Car	Entertainment	Other
Sept 1	Balance	450	Oct 3	Bus	15.50					15.50
June 2	Wages	480	Oct 3	Groceries	198	198				
Oct 1	Balance	500	Oct 5	Coal	30					30
Oct 2	Wages	566	Oct 5	Car Insurance	500			500		
Oct 13	Child Benefit	20	Oct 7	Show	80				80	
			Oct 7	take away	50	50				
			Oct 11	Grocery	220	220				
			Oct 11	taxi	12					12
			Oct 12	Petrol	55	55				
			Oct 12	Pocket Money	25					25
	Balance c/d	99.50		Balance c/d						
		1185.50			1185.50					
				Balance B/D	99.50					

10 Answer the following questions using Question 18 on page 42 of the textbook. Complete the statement before answering the questions.

	Budget Jan-Dec	Actual	Difference
Salaries	18,000	18,900	+900
Child benefit	960	1,140	+180
Other		800	+800
Total income	**18,960**	20,840	+1880
Expenditure			
Fixed			
Mortgage	14,400	13,300	−1100
Car insurance	567	550	−17
House insurance	300	350	+50
Subtotal	15,267	14,200	−1067
Irregular			
Household costs	7,540	9,500	+1960
Shoes and clothes	3,000	2,500	−500
Car costs	1,200	1,300	+100
Light and heat	1,800	1,789	−11
Medical expenses	400	500	+100
Subtotal	13,940	15,589	+1649
Discretionary			
Entertainment	1,000	1,200	+0
Gifts	900	700	+0
Subtotal	1900	1900	0
Total expenditure	31107	31,689	2716
Net cash: surplus/deficit	−12147	−10849	−836

(a) Did the Bernie family have a surplus or a deficit at the end of the year? _____Deficit_____

(b) How much was it for: Budget € ____−12147____ and Actual € __−10849___

(c) Difference: € ___−1298_____

(d) Closing balance: € __−836_____

11 Budget comparison statement.

When the Jackson family checked their analysed cash book at the end of December 2013, they discovered that their actual income and expenditure for the 12 months differed from the budgeted figures (contained in the budget comparison statement below) due to the following:

- The salaries of the Jackson family had decreased by 8%.
- They have three children; the child benefit decreased by €5 per child.
- Interest and dividends are €500 less than budgeted.
- They won €500 in the prize bond draw.
- Mortgage payments decreased by €90 per month from 1 April.
- Car insurance increased by €399.
- TV licence price was not changed.
- Household running costs were 11% greater than planned.
- Car costs were €800 greater than expected.
- Light and heat costs increased by 9%.
- Medical expenses were €50 per month.
- Entertainment costs average €120 per month except in June, August and December when they were €140.
- Due to a birthday party, presents cost €120 more than planned.
- They decided to cancel the budgeted holiday and visited Galway for the weekend at a cost of €450.

Complete the following budget comparison statement for the Jackson family.

Income	Budget Jan-Dec €	Actual €	Difference €
Salaries	30,000	− 27600	− 2400
Child benefit	1,200	− 1185	− 15
Interest and dividends	680	− 180	− 500
Other		+ 500	+ 500
Total income	31,880	29,465	− 2415
Expenditure			
Fixed			
Mortgage	4,950	4140	− 810
Car insurance	600	999	+ 399
TV licence	152	152	+ 0
Subtotal	5,702	5291	− 411
Irregular			
Household	17,040	18914.40	+ 1874.40
Car	900	1700	+ 800
Light and heat	2,150	2343.50	+ 193.50
Medical expenses	450	600	+ 150
Subtotal	20,540	23557.90	+ 3017.90
Discretionary			
Entertainment	1,320	1500	+ 180
Presents	390	510	+ 120
Holidays	1,100	450	− 650
Subtotal	2,810	2460	− 950
Total expenditure	29,052	31308.90	4378.90
Net cash	3,467	−1843.90	−1963.90
Opening cash	900	4367.00	900
Closing cash	4,367	2523.10	1063.90

Communication

Exercises Based on Chapter Content

1 Fill in the following chart with examples of different types of communication.

Visual	Oral	Written
Pie Chart	Telephone	email
Line graph	Lecture	Blog
Bar chart	Class	report
Film	Podcast	Memo

2 List and explain the factors that are looked at when choosing a method of communication.

1. Cost - How expensive its to send   2. Speed - How Fast does message travel
3. Secrecy - Who'll Know Whats in the message
4. Distance - How Far Must the message be sent
5. Record - Is there a need to have a record of message

3 Indicate three methods each for external and internal communication.

Internal communication	External communication
Memo	Fax
Intercom	Phone
Meetings	Internet

4 Assume that you are secretary of the School Council. Draft a memo to all students of your school telling them that voting for the School Council will take place on Monday morning at assembly. Voting will end at 9.30am and there is one vote per student.

To: All Students in the School
From: School Secretary
Date: 13/5/12
Re: Voting For School Council

I am telling you all about voters For the school council will take place on Monday Morning in assembly and there's one Vote Per student. Voting will end at 9:30 A.M.

Yours Sincerly
School Secretary

5 Write a letter to your local county/city council asking for an application form for a dog licence. Use your own address and today's date.

6 Fill in the missing headings in the following checklist used when writing business letters.

Your address	OAH	Their address	Salutation	Re:	Parts of Letter	Closure	Signature	Enclosure
1	2	3	4	5	6,7,8,9	10	11	12
✔	✔	✔	✔	✔	✔	✔	✔	✔

7 Draft the reply sent by Robert Charlton, Manager of Trá Bán Hotel, to D'Arcy Blinds Ltd (see page 48 of the textbook), confirming the booking, repeating the details from the letter and enclosing a receipt for the deposit.

8 Fill in the blank headings for the following report.

Lateness Issue Raised at Recent Staff Meeting

To
_____: Staff of Alexander School

From
_____: Principal

Re:
_____: To write a report on why students from Marygoggin are 15-20 minutes late for school Monday to Thursday.

Dear   Staff

I spoke with a sample of students and their parents about the lateness.

Salutation

I am informed that broadband works involving St Martin's Road start at 8.30. This results in traffic delays of up to 25 minutes.

The works do not start until 9.30 on Friday and Saturday. The works are supposed to end in two weeks.

Closure   :

This problem will be sorted by the end of this month.

Enclosure   :

That the school does not make an issue of late coming for the next two weeks.

Signed
Mary Barrett
Mary Barrett – Principal

9 Draft a pie chart, line graph or bar chart for the following information.

(a) 660 students – 40% male.

(b) 200 customers for hotel – 20% order breakfast and dinner; 60% order breakfast only; the balance order no food.

(c) The price of monthly mobile phone top-up in the last year for three mobile phone companies are as follows:

Jan	Feb	March	April	May	June	July	Aug	Sept	Oct	Nov	Dec
20	25	25	25	25	25	30	30	30	30	35	35
25	25	25	25	30	30	35	35	35	40	40	40
15	15	25	25	25	30	30	30	35	35	40	40

The Consumer

1. What is the NCA?

The National Consumer agency. It is in charge of defending consumer ~~rights~~ interest and Promoting Consumer rights.

2. Complete the following sentences. The Sale of Goods and Supply of Services Act 1980 states that goods sold or rented must:

   - Be of ' Merchantable quality'.
   - Be fit for the Purpose .
   - Conform to (be like) the Sample shown.
   - Be as described by the shop, packet, or adverts.

3. Name the three R's.

   (a) Refunds (b) Replacements (c) Repair

4. Name the card that helps consumers to know their rights. Shoppers rights Card

5. Fill in the blanks in the following sentences.

   How to complain if goods are not right:

   If you have a problem you should Contact the shop as soon as possible. A letter giving all the details is a good method. You can also phone, e-mail or call into the Shop .

   State the problem _____.

6 Examine the following letter of complaint. Fill in the missing items.

Hampton's Department Store
Patrick Street, Cork

VAT no. IT2398745
24 February 2011

Rene Digital Camera
RI44   €195.00

TOTAL DUE   €195.00
Cash   €195.00
Change   0.00

5 Archer Drive
Gibbinstown
Dublin 22

24 - February 2011

Mr J. Carolan

Manager

Hampton's Department Store
Patrick Street
Cork

_*RE*_ : Complaint – faulty camera

_*Dear*_____ Mr Carolan

On Saturday last, February 24, I purchased a Rene Digital Camera _*(model R144)*_.

I have enclosed a copy of the _*till recept*_.

On examination of the camera at home, I found that the _*Shutter didn't work*_

properly. The camera is not fit _*For the Purpose*_ intended, nor is it of

*Merchantable quality*. Therefore, I would appreciate a cash refund.

I hold the item for your collection and await hearing from you.

Yours _*Faithfully*_

Charles T. Bronson

Charles T. Bronson

Encl. 1

7 Fill in the Small Claims Court form using the following information and Question 6 on the previous page. Charles Bronson (phone number 01 98765432) was ignored by the shop (phone number 01 23456789). They did not answer his letter nor return his phone calls. He decided to use the Small Claims Court. Assume that you are Charles Bronson.

Form 53A.1

Order 53A r3

Claim No.

AN CHÚIRTE DUICHE   **THE DISTRICT COURT**

District Court Area of _Gibbinstown Co-Dublin_   District No. _22_

District Court (Small Claims Procedure) Rules, 1999

APPLICATION TO SMALL CLAIMS REGISTRAR

CLAIMANT: Name and address of person making claim	**RESPONDENT:** Name and address of person against whom the claim is made
Charles T. Bronson, 5 Archer Drive, Gibbinstown. Dublin 22	_J. Carolan, Manager, Hamptons department Store. Patrick Street, Co. Cork_
Phone No: _01 98765432_	Phone No: _01 23456789_

CLAIM

Amount claimed: € _195_

Particulars of claim:

The shutter on the camera didn't work. The camera is not fit for the purpose intended.

I hereby apply to have the claim processed through the Small Claims Procedure in accordance with the provisions of the above mentioned Rules

To:
The Small Claims Registrar
District Court Office

Dated this   day of   20

_____
Signature of the person making the claim

Note: This application must be accompanied by a fee of €15

CHAPTER 7

People at Work

1   Explain the following terms.

     (a) Labour force: Labour Force is the total amount OF People that are available For employment.

     (b) Unemployment: happens When Members OF the Labour Force Can't Find Work..

2   **(a)** Distinguish between work and employment.

     Work: Is doing a Job and Not getting Paid For It

     Employment: Is doing a Job and getting Paid For It

     (b) List three factors that encourage employment in the country.

       (i)   Low Interest rates

       (ii)   Low, tax rates e.g Income and corporation tax.

       (iii)   A highly educated and trained WorkForce.

3   Look up the Central Statistics Office website (www.cso.ie) and answer the following questions using the most recent figures.

     (a) Total in employment: _____

     (b) Total unemployed: _____

     (c) Total labour force: _____

     (d) Compare each of these answers with the table on employment and unemployment in the textbook (page 69) and comment on the trend in each case.

4   List four possible causes of unemployment.

     (a) A decline in traditional industries Such as clothing + Farming

     (b) High Labour Costs

     (c) New technology and automated Processes

     (d) A recession in Ireland or abroad

5 **(a)** Name two sources of assistance for the unemployed, and briefly explain each.

(i) Area Partnership Companies that encourage Job creation and enterprise among the unemployed

(ii) FÁS they provide training For School Leavers and the unemployed

(b) Identify two possible consequences for Ireland of having a high unemployment rate.

(i) Emigration

(ii) A decrease In Social Welfare Payments

6 **(a)** List and explain three levels of employee skills.

(i) unskilled - Have no Formal training or qualification

(ii) Semi-skilled - Employees who have been trained in a Particular task

(iii) Skilled - People with a recognized job skill qualification

(b) Identify two examples for each of the following job categories.

(i) Manual: Labourer + Plasterer

(ii) Clerical: typist + bank teller

(iii) Technical: Chemist + Programmer

(iv) Creative: Artists + Writers

(v) Services: Doctor + Hairdresser

(vi) Administrative: Supervisor + Manager

7 Briefly explain the role of FÁS.

The Provide training For School Leavers and the unemployed. It also Provides Social employment Schemes.

8 Tick the boxes (✔) to indicate **true** or **false**.

	True	False
(a) A hairdresser works in the services sector.	✔	
(b) A machine operator is an example of semi-skilled labour.	✔	
(c) Everyone working in construction is an example of manual labour.		✔
(d) A computer programmer is a semi-skilled technical employee.		✔
(e) A fashion designer is an artistic/creative job.	✔	

9 Identify two functions of each of the following departments in a company.

(a) Marketing: _Carries out Market research, advertising + sales Promotion. Responsible_ _for selling the goods/services to the consumer_

(b) Human resources: _Responsible for hiring + firing. Deals with_ _industrial relations issues._

(c) Accounts: _Keeps the financial accounts + Manages bank records_

10 **(a)** List two benefits of having an organisation structure in the workplace.

(i) _It sets up a chain of command_

(ii) _It delegates work + responsibility._

(b) Complete the organisational chart of a limited company which has four departments.

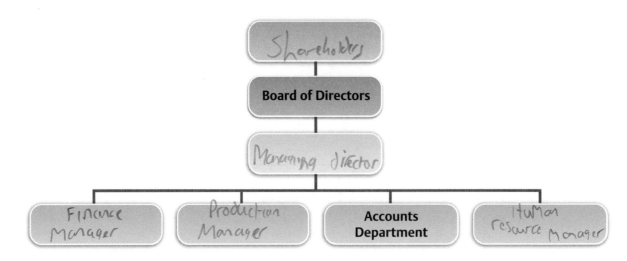

Shareholders

Board of Directors

Managing director

Finance Manager | Production Manager | **Accounts Department** | Human resource Manager

11 Match the job title below with the correct job description.

A	Accountant	**1**	Encourages the public to buy the firm's products/services.
B	Managing Director	**2**	Types letters, files, answers the telephone, etc.
C	Salesperson	**3**	Keeps a register of shareholders, ensures company abides by laws, etc.
D	Company Secretary	**4**	Manages the accounts department.
		5	In charge of the company on a day-to-day basis.

A	B	C	D
4	3 5	1	2

12 Draw an organisation structure for a sole trader employing thirteen employees as follows: two supervisors, ten machine operators and one secretary/receptionist.

13 Draw an organisation structure for a private limited company with four departments – Production, Purchasing/Stores, Marketing, Accounts.

14 Draw an organisation structure for a department store with four departments, each with an assistant manager in charge. Each department employs the following:
- Grocery – two supervisors and twelve shop assistants.
- Electrical – three shop assistants.
- Clothing (two sections) – Male: two shop assistants; Female: two shop assistants.
- Household – three shop assistants.

15 Explain the following terms.

(a) Shareholders: owns shares in the company. They usually have one vote for each share. Receive a dividend if company is profitable.

(b) Board of Directors: Sets the aims + objectives of the company. They try to run the company profitably + provide good return to shareholder.

(c) Managing Director: Runs the company on a day to day basis. Responsible for achieving objectives of a company. Appoints senior management + delegates responsibility + authority

(d) Company Secretary: Keeping a shareholder register. Making sure company obeys its own rules.

16 Outline three rights and three responsibilities of being an employee.

Rights:

(a) A Fair days work For a Fair days Wage

(b) To be in safe + Proper Conditions

(c) to join a trade union IF they wish

Responsibilities:

(a) Doing a Fair days work

(b) Not stealing or damaging From the employer

(c) to be loyal

17 (a) Write a brief note on self-employment.

A Person who owns + runs the business. Takes the risk of going into the business to Provide a good /service with the risk OF Possible Failure or Loss.

(b) Identify two examples of self-employed people from your own area.

(i) 'Dalys' sweet shop

(ii) OFFaly driving school

(c) Outline three benefits and three drawbacks of being self-employed.

Benefits:

(i) Your are Your own boss + Make Your own descisions

(ii) You can keep the Profit

(iii) Decide on Product/service to sell

Drawbacks:

(i) Business could Fail + you could lose Your Money + Job

(ii) ProFit May be Low

(iii) May have to work very Long hours

18 **(a)** Explain the following terms.

(i) Redundancy: Being let go? because theres no more work available

(ii) HRM: _____

(iii) Factors of production: There are 4 Factors of Production. Land, Labour, Capital, enterprise

(b) Outline two economic effects of a growing labour force.

(i) That there Would Not be enough Jobs For everyone of them.

(ii) Higher output and a higher Gross National Product

_____

Being an Employer

1 Complete your curriculum vitae (CV) using the following layout.

CURRICULUM VITAE

Name: _____

Address: _____

_____

_____

Phone No.: _____

EDUCATION
Primary School: _____

Dates: _____

Secondary School: _____

Dates: _____

QUALIFICATIONS
Junior Certificate [Date:]

Subjects	**Level**	**Grade**

Leaving Certificate [Date:]

Subjects	**Level**	**Grade**

WORK EXPERIENCE

Dates	Name of Workplace	Description
_____	_____	_____
		_____
_____	_____	_____
		_____

INTERESTS & HOBBIES

➢

➢

➢

➢

SKILLS

➢

➢

➢

ACHIEVEMENTS

➢

➢

REFEREES

Name: _____   Name: _____

Position: _____   Position: _____

Address: _____   Address: _____

_____   _____

_____   _____

Phone No. _____   Phone No. _____

Signature: _____   Date: _____

2 **(a)** List three suitable media for advertising a job vacancy.

(i) _____

(ii) _____

(iii) _____

(b) Outline four steps that you should take when preparing for an interview.

(i) _____

(ii) _____

(iii) _____

(iv) _____

3 List three rights and three responsibilities of being an employer.
Rights:

(a) _____

(b) _____

(c) _____

Responsibilities:

(a) _____

(b) _____

(c) _____

4 Explain the following terms.

(a) Induction: _____

_____

(b) Contract of employment: _____

_____

(c) Job description: _____

_____

5   Examine the job advertisement (from the *Daily Post* on today's date) and answer the questions below.

> ### Restaurant Manager Required
> A restaurant in Cobh is seeking a suitable candidate to manage the restaurant. The ideal candidate should have appropriate qualifications and experience in the food industry. The manager will need to have leadership abilities and organisational skills.
>
> For further details and an application form please write to: Mr John O'Driscoll, Seaview, Cobh, Co. Cork.
>
> **An Equal Opportunities Employer**

(a) Other than a newspaper, name two other suitable media for advertising this position.

(i) _____

(ii) _____

(b) List four details contained in a CV.

(i) _____

(ii) _____

(iii) _____

(iv) _____

(c) Write a letter requesting an application form, and further details about the job, using today's date.

(d) Explain the term 'equal opportunities employer': _____

_____

_____

6   Calculate the gross pay for each of the following.

(a) €12.50 per hour. Worked 38 hours.	**(b)** €7.50 per item. Made 50 items.

7 Calculate the gross pay for each of the following.

(a) €14 per hour for a 39-hour week. Overtime at 'time and a half'. Worked 42 hours.

(b) Basic pay €360 plus 8% commission on sales of €3,200.

8 Calculate the gross pay for each of the following.

(a) Sewing 900 garments at 60c per garment.

(b) Insurance salesperson selling €24,000 worth of insurance receiving 7.5% commission.

9 Look at the wages book in Chapter 8 of the textbook (page 80) and answer the following questions.

(a) How much tax is Thomas O'Neill paying? _____

(b) What is the employer's total employment bill for the week? _____

(c) Explain the term 'union subscription': _____

10 Record the following details of three employees into the wages book of Healy Ltd.
(a) Peter Casey: gross wages €720; PAYE €85; PRSI €48.
(b) Jayne Roberts: gross wages €700; PAYE €80; PRSI €45.
(c) Enda Harte: gross wages €780; PAYE €96; PRSI €50.
All employees pay pension at 8% of gross wages. Employers PRSI contribution @10%.

Employee	Work No.	Gross Pay €	Deductions				Employer's PRSI	Total Deductions €	Net Pay €
			PAYE	PRSI	Pension	Union			
P. Casey	1					6			
J. Roberts	2					6			
E. Harte	3					6			
Totals									

11 Record the following details of three employees into the wages book of Refit Ltd.
(a) Mary Healy: gross wages €540; PAYE €48; PRSI 8%.
(b) Wayne Hogan: gross wages €530; PAYE €46; PRSI 8%.
(c) Alex Ryan: gross wages €570; PAYE €54; PRSI 8%.
All employees pay pension at 6% of gross wages. Employer's PRSI contribution @12%.

Employee	Work No.	Gross Pay €	Deductions				Employer's PRSI	Total Deductions €	Net Pay €
			PAYE	PRSI	Pension	Union			
M. Healy	1					5			
W. Hogan	2					5			
	3					5			
Totals									

12 Explain the following terms.

(a) Time rate: _____

_____

(b) Piece rate: _____

_____

(c) Commission: _____

_____

13 Explain the following terms.

(a) Flexitime: _____

_____

(b) Bonus: _____

_____

14 Complete the following payslip using the information contained in Question 16 on page 85 of the textbook.

Week No.		Gross Pay			Deductions				Date	Employee No. ____
Name		Basic	Overtime	Total	PAYE	PRSI	Pension	Union	Total Deductions	Net Pay

15 Complete the following payslip using the information contained in Question 17 on page 85 of the textbook.

Week No.		Gross Pay			Deductions				Date	Employee No. ____
Name	Basic	Overtime	Total	PAYE	PRSI	Pension	Union	Total Deductions	Net Pay	

16 Pat Broderick (work no. 12) worked a 39-hour week @ €15 per hour. On the week ending 9 March 2013 (week 10) Pat also worked 5 hours overtime at 'time and a half', and 2 hours at 'double time'. Pat's PAYE was €84, PRSI €56, pension €70 and trade union subscription €6. Complete the payslip for the week ending 9 March 2013.

Week No.		Gross Pay			Deductions				Date	Employee No. ____
Name	Basic	Overtime	Total	PAYE	PRSI	Pension	Union	Total Deductions	Net Pay	

17 Jim O'Brien (work no. 2) worked a 36-hour week @ €18 per hour. On the week ending 16 March 2013 (week 11) Jim also received commission of €240. His PAYE was €110, PRSI €63 and pension €89. Jim is not a member of a trade union.

Week No.		Gross Pay			Deductions				Date	Employee No. ____
Name	Basic	Commission	Total	PAYE	PRSI	Pension	Union	Total Deductions	Net Pay	

(a) Complete the payslip for the week ending 16 March 2013.
(b) State two ways in which Jim could benefit from joining a trade union.

(i) _____

(ii) _____

18 Paul O'Driscoll worked a 38-hour week @ €16 per hour. On the week ending 24 April 2013 Paul also received commission of 5% of sales valued at €3,400. His PAYE rate is 20%, his annual tax credit €3,660, PRSI at 8%, savings €25 and trade union €7.50. He also pays the 2% income levy on income over €300 a week. Complete his payslip.

Week No. 16	Gross Pay			Deductions						Date 24/04/2013	Employee no. 45A
Name	Basic	Commission	Total	PAYE	PRSI	Levy	Savings	Union	Total Deductions	Net Pay
Paul O'Driscoll										

Workings:

19 Explain the following terms.

(a) Overtime: _____

(b) Tax credit: _____

(c) Income levy: _____

(d) P60: _____

20 Calculate the annual take home pay of each of the following people. Tax bands (single person): the first €36,400 of income @ 20% and the balance @ 41%.

(a) Kevin O'Regan earns €48,000. His tax credits: €3,660.

(b) Alison Farrell earns €62,500. Her tax credits: €3,660. Income levy 2% on amounts over €15,000.

21 Calculate the annual take home pay of each of the following. Tax bands (single person): the first €36,400 of income @ 20% and the balance @ 41%.

(a) Mark Lyons earns €72,400. His tax credits: €3,900.

(b) Jennifer Ryan earns €54,100. Her tax credits: €3,900. Income levy 2% on amounts over €15,000.

22 Complete the following cash analysis for a business preparing their payroll.

Employee	Net Pay €	€200	€100	€50	€20	€10	€5	€2	€1	50c	20c	10c	5c	2c	1c
M. Costelloe	621.45														
G. Tobin	568.86														
P. Dolan	637.39														
Totals															

23 Complete the following cash analysis for a business preparing their payroll.

Employee	Net Pay €	€200	€100	€50	€20	€10	€5	€2	€1	50c	20c	10c	5c	2c	1c
J. Byrnes	849.77														
A. Grogan	788.39														
B. Lowry	817.68														
Totals															

24 A business has three employees, each paid monthly, who pay PRSI at the rate of 8%. The employer's PRSI is 12%. Each employee also contributes 10% of their gross wages to a pension fund and pays €20 per month in trade union subscriptions. Complete the wages book.

Employee	Work No.	Gross Pay €	Deductions				Employer's PRSI €	Total Deductions €	Net Pay €
			PAYE	PRSI	Pension	Union			
C. Connors	1	3,200	340						
D. Higgins	2	3,440	388						
E. Dixon	3	3,600	420						
Totals									

25 Outline three benefits you might receive from PRSI contributions.

(a) _____

(b) _____

(c) _____

Industrial Relations

1 **(a)** Good industrial relations means _____

_____

(b) What factors are likely to give rise to good industrial relations?

(i) _____

(ii) _____

(iii) _____

2 Explain the following terms.

(a) Trade union: _____

_____

(b) Shop steward: _____

_____

3 List three functions of a trade union.

(a) _____

(b) _____

(c) _____

4 Write out in full the name of each of the following trade unions and identify each type, e.g. craft, general etc.

	Trade Union	Type
ASTI		
SIPTU		
IBOA		
INO		
INTO		
MSF		
TUI		
ATGWU		

5 Outline four possible causes of industrial relations disputes.

(a) _____

(b) _____

(c) _____

(d) _____

6 Outline the role of each of the following people.

(a) Shop steward: _____

(b) Rights commissioner: _____

7 Tick the boxes (✔) to indicate **true** or **false**.

	True	False
(a) The FAI is a trade union.		
(b) Equality officers investigate discrimination.		
(c) The LRC attempts to resolve industrial relations disputes.		
(d) Peaceful picketing is now illegal.		
(e) IBEC is the employer representative body.		
(f) Discrimination by age is legal.		

8 Outline the role of each of the following.

(a) Equality officer: _____

(b) ICTU: _____

9 Explain the following terms.

(a) Work to rule: _____

_____

(b) Official strike: _____

_____

(c) Conciliation: _____

_____

(d) Arbitration: _____

_____

10 The bar chart opposite shows the main causes of strikes in a certain industry.
Total days lost = 24,000 days.

(a) How many days were lost due to the following.

  (i) Pay issues: _____

  (ii) Conditions: _____

  (iii) Dismissal: _____

(b) Why might a dispute take place due to:

  (i) Redundancy: _____

  (ii) Demarcation: _____

(c) Draft a pie chart to illustrate the information shown in the bar chart.

11 Draft a pie chart to illustrate the following information.
Total strike days lost = 12,800
Causes: pay = 40%; working conditions = 25%; redundancy = 20%; dismissal = 15%.

12 **(a)** Explain the term 'labour force'. _____

(b) Explain the 'national wage agreement'. _____

_____

_____

13 **(a)** Outline briefly the procedure a trade union must follow in order to officially go on strike.

_____

_____

_____

_____

_____

_____

(b) Describe two methods by which an industrial relations dispute can be resolved.

(i) _____

_____

(ii) _____

_____

(c) Distinguish between conciliation and arbitration. _____

_____

14 **(a)** Explain the headline:

Unemployment rate now 12.5%

_____

_____

(b) Outline two implications for the economy of having a high unemployment rate.

(i) _____

(ii) _____

(c) Name one organisation that assists the unemployed and briefly describe its activities.

_____

_____

_____

_____

15 **(a)** Explain each of the underlined terms in the following article.

Pay cut: _____

_____

> As a result of the recent recession many workers have had to accept one or more of the following cutbacks: <u>pay cuts</u>, going on a <u>3-day week</u>, losing their additional benefits ('<u>perks</u>'), and in some cases <u>redundancy</u>.

3-day week: _____

_____

Perks: _____

_____

Redundancy: _____

_____

(b) Name and explain two methods of calculating the wages of workers.

(i) _____

(ii) _____

(c) Name two statutory deductions from workers' wages, and outline the purpose of each.

(i) _____

(ii) _____

16 **(a)** The Employment Equality Act 1998 makes it illegal to discriminate at work on the following grounds.

(i) _____   **(ii)** _____   **(iii)** _____

(iv) _____   **(v)** _____   **(vi)** _____

(vii) _____   **(viii)** _____   **(ix)** _____

(b) Briefly describe the main points of the Protection of Young Persons (Employment) Act 1996.

_____

_____

_____

_____

17 **(a)** Outline the role of the Human Resource Manager.

_____

_____

_____

(b) Explain the following terms, and give one example of when each might occur.

    (i) Token stoppage: _____

    _____

    (ii) Unofficial strike: _____

    _____

18 The following table shows the number of strikes that occurred in a country over a number of years.

Year	2009	2010	2011	2012	2013
No. of strikes	46	62	38	29	25

(a) Illustrate the above information on a suitable chart or graph.

(b) Calculate the average number of strikes for the period 2009–2013. _____

(c) Suggest one possible reason why the annual number of strikes is decreasing between 2010 and 2013.

_____

(d) Outline two possible methods of resolving industrial relations disputes.

    (i) _____

    _____

    (ii) _____

    _____

(e) Name one state organisation involved in resolving disputes, and briefly describe its functions.

_____

_____

_____

Sole Trader and Limited Company

Exercises Based on Chapter Content

1 Fill in the blanks in the following statements.

Advantages of a sole trader	Disadvantages of a sole trader
Own boss	If the business goes _____ (owe more _____ money than you have) you will lose _____ and also lose your house, car, furniture ... everything.
All _____	Unlimited _____
Make all business _____ e.g. opening time.	Sole trader must be an expert in all areas of business – stocktaking, keeping accounts etc.
	Shortage of _____ (capital) makes it difficult _____ expand.

2 Give four examples of sole traders.

(a) _____

(b) _____

(c) _____

(d) _____

3 Fill in the blanks in this paragraph about a limited company.

Some facts about _____ Company

■ A company needs at least two people to _____; it may have one owner but needs two

_____ People who invest in a company are called _____

■ People buy shares for two reasons:

(a) The _____ at the end of the year is _____ between the shareholders.

(b) Each share allows one _____ at meetings.

■ The more shares owned the _____ the say in the running of the company.

4 What is the authorised capital of a private company? _____

5 Name the person elected by shareholders to run the company. _____

6 What is the function of the Board of Directors? _____

_____

_____

7 What is the formula for calculation of dividend?

8 Calculate the dividend per share in each of the following cases.

Net profit €	Number of shares	Dividend per share
89,000	100,000	
56,000	200,000	
96	250,000	
900	1,000,000	

Co-operatives and Semi-state Bodies

Exercises Based on Chapter Content

1   What is a co-operative? _____

_____

2   In your opinion, what is the biggest advantage of being a member of a co-operative?

_____

_____

3   Where was the first co-operative in Ireland founded? _____

Who founded it? _____

4   Explain the common bond (in credit union members). _____

_____

5   Fill in the blanks in the following sentences.

Advantages of being in a credit union

■ Any _____ saved with a credit union is automatically covered by a life assurance of €1 for every €1 saved.

■ If the saver dies with €2,000 saved, the next of kin will get €_____.

■ All loans are covered by life _____ and are paid off by this if the borrower dies. The loan

_____ with the borrower.

6   List three reasons why the government is involved in semi-state enterprise.

(a) _____

(b) _____

(c) _____

7 Many semi-state bodies are known by their initials. Write out in full the names of the following examples.

(a) CIE: _____ – provides rail, bus and train transport.

(b) FÁS: _____ – training authority. Training and retraining workers.

(c) CERT: _____ – train staff for the catering/service sector.

(d) RTÉ: _____ – communication, television and radio service.

(e) DART: _____ – rail system serving the coastal areas of Dublin city.

(f) EPA: _____ – maintain and improve the Rivers, Lakes, Land, Forests Act and is on constant watch for pollution.

(g) NTMA: _____ – overall control of the government's borrowing and repayment of loans. Looks for the best rates and value.

8 What is the function of the following commercial semi-state bodies?

(a) VHI (Voluntary Health Insurance): _____

(b) Bord Gáis: _____

(c) Aer Rianta: _____

(d) National Lottery: _____

(e) ESB (Electricity Supply Board): _____

(f) An Post: _____

Insurance

1 List and explain four principles of insurance.

(a) _____

_____

(b) _____

_____

(c) _____

_____

(d) _____

_____

2 A house is currently valued at €250,000 for insurance purposes. However, the home owner has only insured the house for €200,000. A fire in the kitchen has caused €10,000 worth of damage according to the insurance assessor (loss adjuster).

(a) What is an insurance assessor (loss adjuster)? _____

_____

(b) How much compensation will the home owner receive? Explain your answer. _____

_____

3 A house valued at €220,000 is destroyed by fire. The assessor was informed by the fire report that the thatch roof caught fire during renovation work. The house is fully insured but the owner neglected to mention the thatch roof, as it was not asked on the proposal form.

(a) What is a proposal form? _____

_____

(b) How much compensation will the home owner receive? Explain your answer. _____

_____

_____

_____

4 Explain the following terms.

(a) Premium: _____

_____

(b) Loading: _____

_____

5 In the textbook (page 107) there are three quotations – SAFE Insurance, ARC Insurance and CHESTER Insurance. If a house rebuilding cost is valued at €280,000 and the contents valued at €40,000, calculate the premium in each case.

SAFE Insurance plc	ARC Insurance plc	CHESTER Insurance plc

6 An insurance company quotes the following rates for house insurance: buildings @ €1.60 per €1,000; and contents @ €2.25 per €1,000. Calculate the premium each of the following home owners would pay.

Buildings: €160,000 Contents: €26,000	Buildings: €540,000 Contents: €90,000	Buildings: €220,000 Contents: 20% of buildings

7 An insurance company quotes the following rates for house insurance.
   Urban: buildings @ €1.50 per €1,000; and contents @ €2.40 per €1,000.
   Rural: buildings @ €1.40 per €1,000; and contents @ €2.00 per €1,000.
Calculate the premium each of the following home owners would pay.

Buildings: €180,000 (city) Contents: €32,000	Buildings: €300,000 (rural) Contents: €50,000	Buildings: €610,000 (city) Contents: €75,000

8 Explain the following terms.

(a) Actuary: _____

_____

(b) Days of grace: _____

_____

(c) Third party motor insurance: _____

_____

9 Mary Peters, a nurse who is 26 years old and single, lives at 14 The Manse, Gorey, Co. Wexford. The house is a six-year-old, three-bedroomed, semi-detached two-storey house which Mary bought one year ago. Mary has a mortgage of €160,000 with the Bank of Ireland, Main Street, Gorey. The house has two smoke alarms and has a monitored alarm system. Mary's house insurance is currently with Allianz. She wishes to insure the building for €180,000 and the contents for €40,000. An insurance company has quoted her the following rates:

Buildings: €1.25 per €1,000; contents: €2.00 per €1,000.
Discount: 5% for smoke alarms; 15% for monitored burglar alarm.

(a) Complete the following proposal form.

HOUSE INSURANCE
PROPOSAL FORM

Personal Details

Name: _____ Email: _____

Address: _____

_____

Telephone: Home _____ Work _____ Mobile: _____

Occupation: _____ Position: _____

Age: _____

Number of years at present address: _____ Have you a mortgage? Yes/No

If yes, what is the name of the mortgage provider: _____ Address _____

_____

Amount: € _____

House Details

Type of Building: Detached house ☐ Detached bungalow ☐
Semi-detached ☐ Terraced ☐

Number of stories: _____ Number of bedrooms: _____ Age of building: _____

Is there? A burglar alarm: Yes/No A smoke alarm: Yes/No

Amount of insurance cover required: Buildings € _____

Contents € _____

Is the dwelling left unoccupied regularly? Yes/No

Do you currently have house insurance? Yes/No

If yes, please give details: _____

Declaration

I declare that to the best of my knowledge all statements and particulars with regard to this proposal are true and I have not withheld any information relevant to this proposal. This proposal shall form the basis of a contract between me and the insurance company.

Signature of proposer: _____ Date: _____

(b) What principle of insurance applies when completing the proposal form? Briefly explain the principle.

_____

_____

(c) Calculate the premium Mary will have to pay to insure her house and contents.

(d) List, and briefly explain, three factors that can affect the size of the premium.

(i) _____

_____

(ii) _____

_____

(iii) _____

_____

10 Explain the following terms.

(a) Assurance: _____

_____

(b) Average clause: _____

_____

(c) No claims bonus: _____

_____

(d) Endowment life assurance: _____

_____

11 A house is valued at €350,000 but is currently insured for €250,000. A fire in the house results in €56,000 worth of damage according to the assessor (loss adjuster). How much compensation is the home owner entitled to receive and why? Explain your answer.

_____

_____

_____

12 A house is valued at €220,000 but is currently insured for €180,000. A burglary and vandalism of the house results in a loss of €16,500 according to the assessor (loss adjuster). How much compensation is the home owner entitled to receive and why? Explain your answer.

_____

_____

_____

13 A house is currently valued at €250,000 but is insured for €300,000. A water leakage in the house results in damage of €12,000 according to the assessor (loss adjuster). How much compensation is the home owner entitled to receive and why? Explain your answer.

_____

_____

_____

14 Give three reasons why it is important for a business to have adequate insurance cover.

(a) _____

_____

(b) _____

_____

(c) _____

_____

15 Name and briefly explain three insurance policies that you would advise a business to have.

(a) _____

_____

(b) _____

_____

(c) _____

_____

16 A company employing eight staff requested an insurance quotation from an insurance company for the following: buildings €360,000; equipment €90,000; three vehicles €51,000; stock €42,000. The building has smoke alarms and a centrally monitored alarm system.

The insurance company quoted the following:
- Buildings: €1.80 per €1,000.
- Equipment: €2.80 per €1,000.
- Employee liability: €150 per employee.
- Vehicle (comprehensive): €780 per vehicle.
- Stock: €5.20 per €1,000.

Workings

The insurance company also offers a 5% discount for smoke alarms and a 15% discount for a monitored alarm system (excluding employee liability and vehicles).

(a) Calculate the amount of premium the company will have to pay if they accept the quotation.

_____

(b) Name and explain two other insurance policies that the company would be advised to have.

(i) _____

(ii) _____

17 A male, aged 20 years, received the following car insurance quotation. Explain what the three quotations mean and why they differ in price.

Third Party: _____

_____

_____

Car Insurance Quotation

Third Party	€ 950
Third Party, Fire & Theft	€1,100
Comprehensive	€1,400

Third Party, Fire & Theft: _____

_____

_____

Comprehensive: _____

_____

_____

18 James Brady, date of birth 14 April 1983, is a store manager who lives at Apt 4, The Mill, Ennis, Co Clare. He drives a Nissan Primera (1595 cc), registration number 06-CE-759, with full comprehensive insurance (policy CL3476981). On Thursday last at 6.15pm his car was hit from behind by a van after he had stopped at traffic lights. A pedestrian, Mary O'Brien, witnessed the accident and stated to the local Gardaí that James had stopped at a red light but the van failed to stop in time. Fortunately nobody was injured. The back of the car was badly damaged, including the rear light (right-hand side), the rear bumper, the bodywork on the right-hand side and the boot. The main dealer's repair estimate is €3,200. The van driver accepted responsibility and after exchanging insurance details, and being cautioned by the Gardaí, he was free to go.

(a) Complete the insurance claim form for James.

MOTOR ACCIDENT CLAIM FORM

Policy No:_____

Name: _____ Telephone no. (H) _____

(W) _____

Address: _____

_____

Date of birth: _____ Occupation: _____

Vehicle

Make: _____ Model: _____ c.c.: _____

Year of manufacture: _____ Registration no.: _____

Accident

Give full details of damage to the vehicle: _____

_____

Date of accident: _____ Time of accident: _____

Location of accident: _____

Was anybody injured? Circle the appropriate word: Yes/No

If yes, please give details: _____

_____

_____

Describe how the accident occurred: _____

_____

_____

Were the Gardaí notified? Circle the appropriate word. Yes / No

Which Garda Station? _____

Were there witnesses to the accident/damage? Circle the appropriate word. Yes/No

If yes, name of the witness: _____

Address of the witness: _____

_____

Estimated cost of repair: €_____ (Estimates from an approved garage must be attached.)

Driver

Name: _____ Address: _____

_____

Is the driver a named driver for this vehicle? Circle the appropriate word. Yes/No

If no, please give details: _____

Was the driver injured? Circle the appropriate word. Yes/No

Was the driver arrested as a result of the accident? Circle the appropriate word. Yes/No

If yes, please give details _____

Declaration

I declare that the above particulars are true, to the best of my knowledge.

Signed: _____ Date: _____

(b) Will this affect James's 'no-claims bonus'? Explain your answer, and refer to the relevant principle of insurance.

_____

_____

_____

_____

_____

19 Distinguish between the following terms.

(a) Insurable risks and non-insurable risks:

_____

_____

(b) No-claims bonus and loading:

_____

_____

(c) Indemnity and contribution:

_____

_____

(d) Cover note and insurance disc:

_____

_____

20 **(a)** Name two types of insurance required by law. Explain each type.

(i) _____

_____

(ii) _____

_____

(b) A business is given the following insurance quotation (for all the policies in place): basic premium €8,000, loadings 20% of the basic, and deductions 12.5% of basic plus loadings.

(i) Give one example of a loading and one example of a deduction.

_____

_____

(ii) Calculate the total annual premium the business must pay. _____

(iii) Outline three steps that a business could take to possibly reduce their insurance premium.

_____

_____

_____

Marketing

1 Complete the following definitions.

(a) Marketing is _____

_____

_____

(b) Market research is _____

_____

_____

2 Give three pieces of information that market research could provide.

(a) _____

(b) _____

(c) _____

3 Give three reasons for undertaking market research.

(a) _____

(b) _____

(c) _____

4 Give three reasons why market research is important.

(a) _____

_____

(b) _____

_____

(c) _____

_____

5 Explain the following terms.

(a) Desk research: _____

_____

(b) Field research: _____

_____

(c) List three methods of field research used to obtain information.

(i) _____

(ii) _____

(iii) _____

6 Match the following terms with the correct definition.

A	Marketing mix	1	Promotes the image of the business and products.
B	Public relations	2	Registered name of the product/service.
C	Product life cycle	3	Techniques used to encourage the public to buy, e.g. coupons.
D	Import substitution	4	Product, price, place, promotion.
E	Brand name	5	Stages in the growth and sales of a product/service.
		6	Manufacturing a product in Ireland that was previously imported.

A	B	C	D	E

7 Briefly explain each of the 4Ps that make up the marketing mix.

(a) _____

_____

(b) _____

_____

(c) _____

_____

(d) _____

_____

8 Draw the product life cycle diagram, clearly identifying each stage of the life cycle and label each axis. Write a brief note on each of the five stages below.

(a) _____

_____

(b) _____

_____

(c) _____

_____

(d) _____

_____

(e) _____

_____

9 Explain the term 'unique selling point' (USP), and give two possible examples.

USP: _____

_____

Examples: **(a)** _____ **(b)** _____

10 Explain the following terms.

(a) Target market: _____

_____

(b) Brainstorming: _____

_____

(c) Random sampling: _____

_____

11 Design an advertisement for a cake sale that your class is planning to hold in order to raise money for Trócaire. In the advertisement give the date, time and venue of the cake sale, as well as a price list.

12 Your class has started an enterprise selling personalised tee-shirts and picture frames made in school. You have been asked to design an advertisement for the sale of the tee-shirts and picture frames. In the advertisement give a description and price list, as well as the venue and date of the sale.

13 Your class has been asked to organise a branch of the local credit union in the school.

(a) Describe how you would propose finding out the level of student interest in this scheme, and how many potential savers there are.

_____

_____

(b) Design a short questionnaire that could be used to undertake the research.

(c) Assuming it is agreed to go ahead with the credit union, name two advertising media that you would use within the school, and give a reason for each choice.

(i) _____

(ii) _____

(d) Design a suitable informative advertisement for the school credit union.

14 Explain the following terms.

(a) PRO: _____

_____

(b) Sales promotion: _____

_____

15 **(a)** List and explain four factors that have to be considered when planning an advertising campaign.

(i) _____

(ii) _____

(iii) _____

(iv) _____

(b) List and explain four factors that will affect the selling price of a product/service.

(i) _____

(ii) _____

(iii) _____

(iv) _____

16 **(a)** Outline two benefits and two drawbacks associated with having a brand name.

Benefits: (i) _____

(ii) _____

Drawbacks: (i) _____

(ii) _____

(b) List three brand names. _____

(c) Outline two benefits associated with public relations.

(i) _____

_____

(ii) _____

_____

(d) Give two examples of sponsorship deals.

(i) _____

(ii) _____

17 Calculate the profit mark-up and the profit margin for each of the following.

(a) Cost price = €120

Selling price = €180

⇒ Profit = € _____

Profit mark-up	Profit margin

(b) Cost price = €240

Selling price = €336

⇒ Profit = € _____

Profit mark-up	Profit margin

18 Calculate the profit mark-up and the profit margin for each of the following.

(a) Cost price = €16

Selling price = €28

⇒ Profit = € _____

Profit mark-up	Profit margin

(b) Cost price = €420

Selling price = €672

⇒ Profit = € _____

Profit mark-up	Profit margin

19 Calculate the profit mark-up and the profit margin for each of the following.

(a) Cost price = €52

Profit = €41.60

⇒ Selling price = € _____

Profit mark-up	Profit margin

(b) Cost price = €630

Profit = €420

⇒ Selling price = € _____

Profit mark-up	Profit margin

20 Calculate the cost price and the selling price for each of the following.

(a) Profit   =   €90

    Profit mark-up   =   60%

Cost price	Selling price

(b) Profit   =   €520

    Profit mark-up   =   80%

Cost price	Selling price

21 The Managing Director of Windpower Ltd has engaged the services of a market research company, before deciding to go into production, in order to undertake research on the potential size of the market for a domestic wind turbine for generating electricity for households. The Managing Director has the specifications of a prototype wind turbine, and has asked the market research company to base the research on this prototype. He also asks them to research a possible selling price for the product.
The market research company produces the following information:

(i)

Provinces	Munster	Leinster	Connaught	Ulster
Potential annual sales	300	200	350	50

(ii) There is already competition in the market.
(iii) The maximum selling price would be €4,000.
(iv) There is a grant available to householders in the Republic of Ireland, which would reduce their expense.

Based on this information, answer the following questions.

(a) Explain the term 'prototype': _____

_____

(b) Illustrate the above table in the form of a pie-chart.

(c) If householders received a grant of 40%, what would be the net cost to the householder?

(d) If the cost of producing a wind turbine (including delivery) is €2,400, and the company is planning a profit mark-up of 60%, what is the projected selling price?

(e) If the estimated investment needed by the company is €576,000, how many units would need to be sold just to break even?

(f) Write a short report for the Managing Director, on today's date, presenting your findings. Recommend whether Windpower Ltd should go ahead, or not, with production of the wind turbine. Give reasons for your recommendation.

CHAPTER 1

Financial Institutions 1 (Banking)

Exercises Based on Chapter Content

1 What is DIRT? _____

_____

2 What factors are looked at by a wise investor when deciding whether to invest money?

(a) _____ **(b)** _____ **(c)** _____

(d) _____ **(e)** _____

3 The government scheme introduced by the Irish government to secure deposits covers deposits in full.
True ☐   False ☐

4 Give one example of proof of identity. _____

5 Calculate the interest (simple) on the following accounts.

	Principal €	Time (years)	Rate %	Formula / workings	Interest earned €
Rena O'Connor	2,300	5	9		
Bernard McMahon	7,800	2	7		
Aoife Hannon	4,500	4	8		
Tom Baker	7,800	6	5		

6 What is C.A.R.? _____

7 Calculate the compound interest on the following accounts.

	Principal €	Time (years)	Rate %	Formula / workings	Interest earned €
Rena O'Connor	2,300	5	9		
Bernard McMahon	7,800	2	7		
Aoife Hannon	4,500	4	8		
Tom Baker	7,800	6	5		

8 Give two examples of identification (ID) showing a photograph.

(a) _____ **(b)** _____

9 Complete a current account application form using the following details.
Diarmuid Curtin, Church Place, Duagh, Co. Kerry (home telephone number 066 785667; mobile number 085 3443298; e-mail DCurtin@eircom.net) works for Listowel Auto Repairs of Bryan McMahon Road, Listowel, Co. Kerry. He has been working there for seven years and earns €1,200 per month. He was born on 18 August 1984 in Co. Kerry and is single. He has a savings account with Listowel Credit Union and has €2,300 deposited in it.

Current Account Application Form

Personal details
Surname _____
First name _____
Home address _____
_____

Date of birth [_____]
Country of birth [_____]
Marriage status [_____]

Employment details
Occupation _____
Employer's name and address _____
_____

Gross salary per month € [_____]
Length of time in present employment [_____]
Will your income be paid directly into your bank account: Yes/No

Contact details
Home phone no. _____ Mobile phone no. _____
E-mail address _____
Do you hold any other bank accounts? Yes/No
Give details _____
_____

Please open a current account in my name. I certify the accuracy of the above information.

Signed: _____ Date: _____

10 When a bank customer seeks 'overdraft accommodation', what is requested?

_____

_____

11 Complete the following cheque.

Date: 2 March 2011		AIB Bank	43-76-90
To: Travel Books Ltd		MAIN STREET, OOLA, COUNTY LIMERICK	Date _____
For: Books		Pay:	OR ORDER
Balance	8,700	Six hundred and twelve euro	€
Am't Lodged	/	and thirty six cent	RAINFOREST BOOKS LTD.
Total	8,700		
This Cheque	€612.36		Jane Grisham
Bal. Forward	€8,087.64		RAINFOREST BOOKS
0009761		00009761 97429765 34–76–90	

counterfoil/stub   cheque

12 Complete the following sentences using the information from page 138 of the textbook.

■ **Stale cheque:** six months have passed since the cheque was written, and it has not been cashed. It is no

longer worth _____. If you have a stale cheque, it may be reissued by the

_____ or redated if the drawer signs the change.

■ _____: this cheque has a date in the future written on it, and it cannot be cashed until this

date. This is sometimes used as security _____. The seller has a cheque that

he can cash in due course.

■ _____: this cheque carries a date in the past. It encourages the payee (person getting the

money) to _____ the cheque quickly.

■ **Blank cheque:** this cheque, though _____, has something missing, e.g. the date, payee's name

(the person named on the face of the cheque after the word 'pay') or even the amount of money.

■ **Stopped cheque:** the drawer (payer of money) has instructed the bank in writing to hold payment of the

money. There may be a problem with the deal or the cheque may have been stolen.

13 Complete the following direct debit form using the following information.

Nora O'Connor wishes to pay the family electricity bill by direct debit. She banks with National Irish Bank, 89 Ryan St, Letterkenny, Co. Donegal. She has a current account. The account number is 9823067. The sort code is 904511. Her telephone number is 086 7744009. Use today's date.

Electricity Company Direct Debit Instruction

I wish to pay the electricity bill by direct debit every month.

To: The Manager

Bank: _____

Bank address: _____

I give permission to the electricity company to charge variable amounts to my bank account.

Name of bank to be debited: _____

Account type: _____

Bank account no.: [_____]

Bank sort code: [_____]

Contact telephone number: [_____]

Signed: _____ **Date:** _____

Financial Institutions 2 (Services Offered)

Exercises Based on Chapter Content

1 List and explain five methods of money transmission offered by banks.

(a) _____

(b) _____

(c) _____

(d) _____

(e) _____

2 Complete the following sentences (the answers can be found on page 145 on your textbook).

ATM (Automated _____ Machine): this is a machine that can _____ money,

_____ phone credit, order statements and check _____ account

_____. They are usually located in busy urban areas, but can also be found in shops and

shopping _____, at concerts, racecourses and even at the National Ploughing Championships.

The customer needs to know their PIN (_____) and, together with their

_____, can withdraw money as suits them.

3 Fill in the following table.

Debit card	Credit card
How does it operate?	How does it operate?
Give an example.	Give an example.

4   Complete the following sentences (the answers can be found on page 146 on your textbook).

Converting to another currency

_____ publish the rate of exchange daily in the _____ section. The figure quoted

is an average of the price _____. That is why the price at the bank counter may differ. Here is an

example of a bank/bureau de change display of currency prices.

Fill in the blanks (*) in the following table.

Euro *_____ Exchange		
	* _____	Buy
Sterling	0.8938	0.904
* _____	1.30	1.32
Japanese yen	127.98	128.98

5   Examine the picture of the 'Western Union Office' on page 147 of your textbook and answer the
following questions.

(a) What is the website address of Western Union? _____

(b) Using the website, find out the cost of sending €200 to London. _____

(c) Look up FEXCO on the Internet.

(d) What is the connection between FEXCO and Co. Kerry? _____

_____

(e) Why does Ireland need a money transmission service? _____

_____

16 Borrowing for an Individual

Exercises Based on Chapter Content

1 What is the charge for money called? _____

2 Calculate how much must be paid back on a house mortgage of €185,000 at 4% per year over 20 years.

3 Complete the following sentences.

- Short term loan: less than _____.

- _____ term loan: 1–5 years.

- Long term loan: _____ 5 years.

4 What are the real facts of borrowing?

_____

_____

_____

_____

_____

5 Give three examples of collateral.

(a) _____

(b) _____

(c) _____

6 Distinguish between flat rate of interest and true rate of interest.

_____

_____

_____

7 Fill in the blanks in the following table.

Sources of Borrowing

Term	Examples	Type of finance
	Holidays Christmas expenses	Bank overdraft Credit union
Medium term loans (1–5 years)		Term loan Hire purchase Leasing (rental)
Long term loans Over 5 years	House purchase	

8 List three rights of a borrower.

(a) _____

(b) _____

(c) _____

9 List five factors that have to be examined before granting loans.

(a) _____

(b) _____

(c) _____

(d) _____

(e) _____

Borrowing for a Company

Exercises Based on Chapter Content

1 Complete the following chart showing the sources of finance that are available to a business. You should learn this chart.

_____-term	_____-term	Long-term
Bank overdraft	Hire _____	_____ earnings
Charge card/company credit card	Leasing	Government assistance/grants
Accrued expenses	Term loan	Long-term loan
_____		Sale _____
Income from sales of stock		Business expansion scheme
_____		_____
Taxation		

2 List three sources of short-term finance.

(a) _____

(b) _____

(c) _____

3 List the rights of a borrower.

(a) _____

(b) _____

(c) _____

4 Name the documents that a business is required to produce when opening a bank account.

(a) _____

(b) _____

(c) _____

Why do you think that this is necessary? _____

_____

5 List the steps involved when a business is applying for a bank loan.

(a) _____

(b) _____

(c) _____

(d) _____

(e) _____

6 Complete the following sentences.
Factors examined before a loan is granted:

■ Is the bank in a position to _____?

■ How _____ is the customer?

■ Is the _____ adequate, i.e. is all the information supplied?

■ How much of the _____ is the lender's (are they putting up some money)?

■ What value of _____ (security) is available?

7 Fill in the following loan application form using the details supplied on page 162 of the textbook.

CE&D Finance Limited

Loan Application Form

Name of Borrower	_____
Address of Borrower	_____
	_____
	_____
Names of Company Directors	_____
	_____
	_____
Nature of Business	_____
Forecasted Annual Income	_____
Amount of Loan Required	€50,000
_____	Up-grade the food preparation area. This is required after a health and safety inspection recommendation by the inspector.
_____	Five years
_____	None
_____	Rita Sullivan
	Michelle Connor
_____	14 February 2012

8 Examine the cash flow forecast for Daithai Ltd on page 163 of the textbook and answer the following questions.

(a) How much opening cash in available? _____

(b) What is the closing balance in August? _____

(c) How much are the total receipts in July? _____

(d) What are the total payments in September? _____

(e) How much is the government grant? _____

9 Examine the loan application for Malloy's Garage Ltd on page 164 of the textbook and answer the following questions.

(a) What is the firm's address? _____

(b) Who is the Managing Director of the firm? _____

(c) Who holds 20% of the shares? _____

(d) When did the firm open for business? _____

(e) What is the NCT? _____

(f) What is the annual sales turnover of the firm? _____

Chain of Production

Exercises Based on Chapter Content

1 Complete the following sentence.

_____ is divided into three areas: primary, _____ and tertiary.

2 List the four types of primary production.

(a) _____   **(b)** _____

(c) _____   **(d)** _____

3 Complete the following paragraph about primary production (see page 168 of the textbook for answers).

Industries involved in primary production are known as _____ industries as they extract the

materials provided by _____ – farming, forestry, fishing and mining. These materials are then

sold to the _____ (e.g. fish, coal, _____) or are used by

industries in _____ and building.

4 Complete the following chains of production.

Milk   Yoghurt, _____, cream.   _____   Flour, bread, _____, bagels.

5 Explain the following terms.

(a) Indigenous: _____

(b) Multinational: _____

6 Complete the following paragraph about tertiary Industry (see page 169 of the textbook for answers).

This industry provides services to _____ and individuals and is known as the service

industry. Businesses need services like _____, warehousing, communications,

_____, computer programming, cleaning and _____. Without these

services, businesses would be unable to operate. The services to individuals include banking, insurance,

legal _____, tax advice, _____, medical, dental and _____.

Channels of Distribution

Exercises Based on Chapter Content

1 How do businesses get their goods to the customer? _____

_____

2 Give an example of a product suitable for each of the channels of distribution shown on page 172 of the textbook.

	2 Channels	3 Channels	4 Channels	5 Channels
Example:				

3 Explain the following terms.

(a) Producer: _____

(b) Manufacturer: _____

(c) Wholesaler: _____

(d) Retailer: _____

4 Complete the following descriptions of retailers.

(a) Sole trader: A retailer who _____ the business. Examples are a coffee shop,

hairdresser, a sports shop or a newsagents. They sometimes offer credit (_____,

_____ later) to loyal local customers.

(b) Supermarket: This is usually a _____ that stocks a variety of goods. It does

not offer _____.

(c) Department store: A shop is divided into many _____ selling different types

of goods. It may also provide _____ services such as a restaurant etc.

(d) _____: This is when a number of small independent retailers join together,

often with a wholesaler, to enable them to compete e.g. Spar, Centra, Daybreak and Londis.

(e) Shopping centre: This is usually located at _____. It comprises many different

stores under one roof and includes parking, restaurants, cinemas, crèches and other facilities.

(f) Mail order firm: When customers buy goods _____ an advertisement

(in a magazine/newspaper). The goods are then sent to customers by post. Credit is usually available.

(g) _____: This specialises in one type of good and carries a large range of this particular

good. Examples are Waterstone's (books), Computer World (computers) and Specsavers (glasses).

(h) Multiple/chain store: This has many branches all over the country, all owned by one single firm. No

_____ is available. They usually stock a range of _____, e.g. different types

of clothes.

5 The following are examples of _____: KFC (Kentucky Fried Chicken), BB's Muffins,

'Who Wants to be a Millionaire', Subway, O'Briens Sandwich Bar and Pizza Hut.

6 List three functions of a retailer.

(a) _____

(b) _____

(c) _____

7 What is EPOST? _____

Delivery Systems

Exercises Based on Chapter Content

1 Draft the diagram showing the journey of the raw material wheat from the raw material producer to the consumer.

2 Outline three advantages of road transport.

(a) _____

(b) _____

(c) _____

3 Tick the appropriate box (✔) to indicate **true** or **false**.

		True	False
(a)	A container is 100ft x 80ft x 40ft.		
(b)	A Sat Nav is nicknamed the 'spy in the cab'.		
(c)	There are five main types of transport in use in Ireland.		
(d)	Sligo has rail access to Dublin.		
(e)	Ennis and Limerick are served by Shannon Airport.		
(f)	Almost 9.8% of Ireland's trade is transported by sea or air.		
(g)	Athlone is a major port.		
(h)	Gas is a suitable product to transport by pipeline.		
(i)	Luas is a light rail system used in Galway city.		
(j)	Ryanair only fly into international airports.		

4 List some of the factors that affect the delivery of goods.

_____

_____

_____

5 Explain the following terms.

(a) CIF: _____

(b) Ex works: _____

(c) FOB: _____

6 Tick the appropriate box (✔) to indicate whether the following costs are fixed or variable for a bus hire company.

	Fixed	Variable
Insurance.		
Wages – bus drivers.		
Toll charges/Easypass.		
Costs of the Tarbert/Killimer car ferry Limerick-Clare.		
Road tax.		

Foreign Trade

1 Match the following terms with the correct description.

A	Visible import	**1**	French tourist in Ireland.
B	Invisible import	**2**	Selling Irish goods abroad.
C	Visible export	**3**	Taxes on imports.
D	Invisible export	**4**	Buying foreign goods in Ireland.
		5	Irish tourist in France.

A	B	C	D

2 Explain the following terms.

(a) Visible import: _____

(b) Invisible import: _____

3 List three reasons why a country needs to import.

(a) _____

(b) _____

(c) _____

4 **(a)** Name three countries that Ireland imports from.

(i) _____ **(ii)** _____ **(iii)** _____

(b) What is the total value of Ireland's imports for the last 12 months (see www.cso.ie)?

_____

5 Explain the following terms.

(a) Visible export: _____

(b) Invisible export: _____

6 List three reasons why a country needs to export.

(a) _____

(b) _____

(c) _____

7 **(a)** Name three countries that Ireland exports to.

(i) _____ (ii) _____ (iii) _____

(b) What is the total value of Ireland's exports for the last 12 months (see www.cso.ie)? _____

8 List two benefits associated with (a) importing and (b) exporting goods/services.

(a) Importing: **(i)** _____

(ii) _____

(b) Exporting: **(i)** _____

(ii) _____

9 Outline three difficulties facing an exporter when selling goods/services abroad.

(a) _____

_____

(b) _____

_____

(c) _____

_____

10 Explain the following terms.

(a) Balance of trade: _____

(b) Balance of trade deficit: _____

11 Outline two methods by which a balance of trade deficit can be corrected.

(a) _____

(b) _____

12 Calculate the balance of trade, based on the following information. Visible imports €43bn. Visible exports €54bn.

13 Calculate the balance of trade, based on the following information. Invisible imports €18bn. Invisible exports €13bn. Visible imports €64bn. Visible exports €68bn.

14 Calculate the balance of trade, based on the following information. Invisible imports €21bn. Invisible exports €19bn. Visible imports €59bn. Visible exports €73bn.

15 Explain the following terms.

(a) Import substitution: _____

_____

(b) Balance of payments on current account: _____

_____

16 The following figures relate to a country's international trade.
Invisible imports €24bn. Invisible exports €17bn.
Visible imports €58bn. Visible exports €76bn.

Workings:

From the above figures:
(a) Calculate the balance of trade. Is there a surplus or a deficit? _____

_____

(b) Calculate the balance of payments (on current account). Is there a surplus or a deficit?

_____

(c) Suggest one thing that consumers could do to help their country's balance of payments.

_____

17 The following figures relate to a country's international trade.
Invisible imports €27bn. Invisible exports €17bn.
Visible imports €62bn. Visible exports €65bn.

Workings:

From the above figures:
(a) Calculate the balance of trade. Is there a surplus or a deficit?

_____

(b) Calculate the balance of payments (on current account). Is there a surplus or a deficit?

_____

18 **(a)** Explain the term 'free trade'. _____

(b) Outline two methods by which the EU can restrict trade with non-EU countries.

(i) _____

(ii) _____

(c) List two benefits resulting from import substitution.

(i) _____

(ii) _____

19 **(a)** Name three countries that are members of the eurozone.

(i) _____ (ii) _____ (iii) _____

(b) Outline three benefits to Irish businesses of being a eurozone member state.

(i) _____

(ii) _____

(iii) _____

20 Convert the following currencies using the foreign currency table.

Euro Rate of Exchange		
	Sell	Buy
Sterling (£)	0.85	0.88
US dollar ($)	1.38	1.42
Japanese yen (¥)	133.45	138.95
Polish zloty	4.06	4.32

(a) €600 into US dollars. _____

(b) €28,000 into sterling. _____

(c) £21,120 into euro. _____

21 Convert the following currencies using the foreign currency table in Question 20.

(a) 1,667,400 Japanese yen into euro. _____

(b) €6,000 into Polish zloty. _____

(c) $23,430 into euro. _____

22 Convert the following currencies using the foreign currency table.

Euro Rate of Exchange		
	Sell	Buy
Sterling (£)	0.88	0.91
US dollar ($)	1.35	1.39
Japanese yen (¥)	131.6	136.8
Polish zloty	4.1	4.3

(a) €21,000 into Polish zloty. _____

(b) €52,000 into sterling. _____

(c) $86,180 into euro. _____

(d) €41,000 into Japanese yen. _____

23 **(a)** Name and briefly describe one institution of the EU. _____

_____

_____

(b) Outline two benefits of EU membership to Irish consumers.

(i) _____

(ii) _____

24 **(a)** When travelling abroad, outline two methods of payment for buying goods or services other than cash.

(i) _____

(ii) _____

(b) Briefly explain one impact that import substitution will have on the balance of trade.

_____

(c) Name, and briefly describe, one state body that encourages Irish exports. _____

_____

_____

(d) Outline two benefits of EU membership to Irish businesses.

(i) _____

(ii) _____

The National Budget

1. Which government department is responsible for preparing the national budget? _____

_____

2. Government income is divided into _____ income and _____ income.

3. List four sources of tax revenue (income) for the government.

   (a) _____   (b) _____

   (c) _____   (d) _____

4. List three possible sources of income for the government other than tax revenue.

   (a) _____   (b) _____   (c) _____

5. List two possible sources of capital income for the government.

   (a) _____   (b) _____

6. Explain the following terms.

   (a) DIRT: _____

   _____

   (b) Corporation tax: _____

   _____

   (c) VAT: _____

   _____

   (d) Stamp duty: _____

   _____

7. Tick the appropriate box (✔) to indicate whether each of the following is current or capital income for the government.

	Current income	Capital income
Privatisation of a semi-state body.		
Stamp duty.		
Borrowing (e.g. ECB).		
Income levy.		
Dividends from semi-state bodies.		

8 Explain the following terms.

(a) National debt: _____

_____

(b) Debt servicing: _____

_____

(c) Privatisation: _____

_____

9 Government expenditure is divided into _____ expenditure and

_____ expenditure.

10 List four examples of the government's current spending.

(a) _____ **(b)** _____

(c) _____ **(d)** _____

11 List two examples of the government's capital spending.

(a) _____ **(b)** _____

12 Tick the appropriate box (✔) to indicate whether each of the following is current or capital expenditure for the government.

	Current expenditure	Capital expenditure
Building a new school.		
Paying teachers' wages.		
Social welfare payments.		
Debt servicing.		
Nationalisation of Anglo Irish Bank.		

13 **(a)** Describe briefly how the national budget is prepared.

(b) Name three groups that watch the budget with interest, and give one reason why each group is affected.

14 **(a)** A budget surplus is _____

(b) A budget deficit is _____

15 List and explain two options facing a government with a current budget deficit.

Option 1: _____

_____

Option 2: _____

_____

16 **(a)** Explain the term 'recession'. _____

_____

(b) List, and briefly explain, three possible effects that a recession can have on the national budget.

(i) _____

_____

(ii) _____

_____

(iii) _____

_____

17 Identify at least one possible effect each of the following would have on the national budget.

(a) Increase in unemployment: _____

(b) Increase in the birth rate: _____

(c) Increase in emigration: _____

18 Identify at least one possible effect each of the following would have on the national budget.

(a) The government nationalising a bank: _____

_____

(b) Increased government borrowing: _____

_____

19 List two economic drawbacks to spending money on capital projects.

(a) _____

(b) _____

20 The following figures were presented on budget day as projections for the year 2013.

Current expenditure	€ million
Social welfare	18,000
Health	15,000
Education	9,000
Debt servicing	7,000
Agriculture	6,000
Other services	15,000
Current revenue (income)	
VAT	20,000
PAYE & income tax	18,000
Excise duties	10,000
Other revenue	12,000

(a) Draft the national budget for 2013 using the above information.

(b) State whether it is a surplus or a deficit budget. _____

21 The following figures were presented on budget day as projections for the year 2013.

Current expenditure	€ million
Social welfare	16,000
Health	8,500
Education	7,500
Debt servicing	7,000
Other services	9,500
Current revenue	
VAT	16,000
Income tax	15,000
Customs & excise	11,000
Other revenue	9,500

(a) Draft the national budget for 2013 using the above information.

(b) State whether it is a surplus or a deficit budget. _____

(c) How would you deal with the surplus/deficit? _____

_____

_____

22 The following figures were presented on budget day as projections for the year 2013.

Current revenue & expenditure	€ million
PAYE	15,260
Debt servicing	8,070
VAT	16,800
Social welfare	13,540
Education	7,900
Corporation tax	3,200
Health services	11,300
Excise duties	1,860
Other revenue	1,100

(a) Draft the national budget for 2013 using the above information.

(b) State whether it is a surplus or a deficit budget. _____

(c) Give two examples of 'other revenue'.

    (i) _____

    (ii) _____

(d) State two options available to a government with a projected surplus deficit.

    (i) _____

    (ii) _____

23 In recent years, unemployment and emigration have increased significantly. List, and briefly explain, two effects each of these could have on the national budget (current account). Are these effects positive or negative?

24 The following figures were presented on budget day as projections for the year 2013.

Current revenue & expenditure	€ million
Debt servicing	6,700
Income tax	16,200
Social welfare	13,500
VAT	15,200
Corporation tax	3,200
Education & science	8,150
Customs & excise duties	2,360
Health services	15,200
Income levy	3,400
Other current expenditure	4,200
Other revenue	4,800

(a) Draft the national budget for 2013 using this information.

(b) State whether it is a surplus or a deficit budget. _____

(c) Give one example of current expenditure and one example of capital expenditure.

Current expenditure: _____

Capital expenditure: _____

25 The following figures were presented on budget day as projections for the year 2013.

Current revenue & expenditure	€ million
Capital income	7,200
Capital expenditure	10,600
Current income	51,000
Current expenditure	45,600

(a) Draft the national budget for 2013 using the above information.

(b) State whether it is a surplus or a deficit budget. _____

(c) The government has decided to increase the capital expenditure on the communications network. Give one economic benefit and one economic drawback to this decision.

Benefit: _____

Drawback: _____

26 The following figures were presented on budget day as projections for the year 2013.

Current revenue & expenditure	€ million
Capital income	6,800
Capital expenditure	11,200
Current income	48,900
Current expenditure	55,800

(a) Draft the national budget for 2013 using the above information.

(b) State whether it is a surplus or a deficit budget. _____

(c) The government has to increase the level of borrowing. Give one economic benefit and one economic drawback to this decision.

Benefit: _____

Drawback: _____

Economic Framework

1 Explain the following terms.

(a) Economics: _____

_____

(b) Limited resources: _____

_____

(c) Opportunity cost: _____

_____

2 **(a)** Distinguish between 'needs' and 'wants'.

Needs: _____

Wants: _____

(b) Explain the term 'financial cost': _____

_____

3 A business has €15,000 to spend and has to decide between upgrading their delivery vans or their computer equipment. The business decides to upgrade the delivery vans.

(a) What is the financial cost involved? _____

(b) What is the opportunity cost involved? _____

4 Explain each of the factors of production.

(a) Land: _____

_____

(b) Labour: _____

_____

(c) Capital: _____

_____

(d) Enterprise: _____

_____

5 Match each factor of production with the appropriate reward paid for it.

Factor of production		Reward	
A	Land	**1**	Interest
B	Labour	**2**	Rent
C	Capital	**3**	Profit
D	Enterprise	**4**	Wage/salary

A	B	C	D

6 Tick the appropriate box (✔) to show the factor of production to which each of the following belongs.

	Land	Labour	Capital	Enterprise
Natural gas				
Equipment				
Secretary				
Vehicles				
Nurse				
Shop owner				
Water				

7 Explain the following terms.

(a) Mixed economic system: _____

_____

_____

(b) Capitalism: _____

_____

_____

8 A farmer has 8 hectares of tillage in which he/she can grow **one** of the following:

(a) 16 tonnes of potatoes @ €350 per tonne; **(b)** 20 tonnes of carrots @ €320 per tonne; or **(c)** 10 tonnes of cabbages @ €420 per tonne.

Which is the best economic choice for the market gardener? _____

_____

What is the opportunity cost? _____

_____

9 Explain the following terms.

(a) Economic growth: _____

_____

(b) Recession: _____

_____

(c) GDP: _____

_____

(d) GNP: _____

_____

10 The following figures are available for a country.
Year 1 GDP = €44 billion.
Year 2 GDP = €45.1 billion.
Calculate the percentage economic growth in the country.

11 The following figures are available for a country.
Year 1 GDP = €52 billion.
Year 2 GDP = €50.7 billion.
Calculate the percentage economic growth/decline in the country.

12 Outline two economic benefits as a result of economic growth in an economy.

(a) _____

_____

(b) _____

_____

13 Outline one drawback associated with economic growth in an economy.

_____

_____

_____

14 Outline two economic consequences of a recession in an economy.

(a) _____

_____

(b) _____

_____

15 Explain the following terms.

(a) Inflation: _____

_____

(b) Deflation: _____

_____

(c) CPI: _____

_____

16 The cost of living 'per capita' in 2011 was €16,000. The cost of living 'per capita' in 2012 was €16,560.

Calculate the rate of inflation.

17 The cost of living 'per capita' in 2012 was €14,600. The cost of living 'per capita' in 2013 was €14,235.

Calculate the rate of deflation.

18 If inflation in Ireland rose by 5%, what likely effect would this have on the following?

(a) Your disposable income: _____

(b) An Irish manufacturer: _____

(c) Your savings earning 1% interest: _____

19 What likely effect would deflation have on each of the following?

(a) Wages: _____

(b) Consumer spending: _____

(c) Exports: _____

20 What likely effect would a recession have on each of the following?

(a) Employment: _____

_____

(b) Government tax revenue: _____

_____

(c) Government spending: _____

_____

21 Draw a line graph to represent the following information.

Year	2009	2010	2011	2012	2013
Inflation	-5%	-2%	1%	4%	3%

(a) If workers do not receive a pay rise in 2010, what effect would this have on their incomes?

_____

(b) Outline two benefits of having low inflation or deflation.

(i) _____

(ii) _____

22 As a result of a recession in the economy, the government have to decrease expenditure and increase borrowing in order to run the country.

(a) Suggest two possible areas where you would effect cutbacks and give one benefit and one drawback of each suggested cutback.

(b) Outline two economic drawbacks associated with cutbacks in spending on the transport system and network.

(c) Instead of borrowing, briefly explain one other source of revenue for the government.

Information Technology

1 Match the following terms with the correct explanation.

1	Hardware	A	Central processing unit.
2	Software	B	Random access memory.
3	ROM	C	Programs (instructions) used in a computer.
4	RAM	D	All the computer equipment.
5	CPU	E	Real optical memory.
6	Modem	F	Read only memory.
		G	Device that converts computer signals to telephone signals.

1	2	3	4	5	6

2 Give three examples of each of the following.

(a) Hardware: _____

(b) Software: _____

3 Give three examples of each of the following.

(a) Input devices: _____

(b) Output devices: _____

4 Name the following parts of the computer.

A: _____

B: _____

C: _____

D: _____

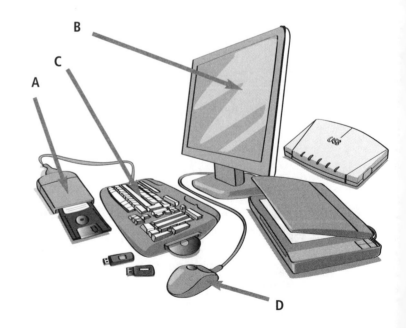

5 Explain the following terms.

(a) Bluetooth device: _____

_____

(b) USB: _____

_____

(c) Operating system: _____

_____

(d) CPU: _____

_____

(e) 1 gigabyte (1GB): _____

_____

6 Explain the following terms.

(a) Mailmerge: _____

_____

(b) CAM: _____

_____

(c) CAD: _____

_____

(d) Desktop publishing: _____

_____

7 List three uses of a computer in the following settings.

(a) At home: **(i)** _____   **(ii)** _____   **(iii)** _____

(b) In business: **(i)** _____   **(ii)** _____   **(iii)** _____

(c) In communications: **(i)** _____   **(ii)** _____   **(iii)** _____

(d) In banking: **(i)** _____   **(ii)** _____   **(iii)** _____

8 Name two input devices that are also output devices.

(a) _____

(b) _____

9 **(a)** With regard to a computer keyboard, fill in the missing letters in the correct order.

Q W _ R _ _

(b) What is the 'caps lock' key used for? _____

(c) What is the 'shift' key used for? _____

10 Explain the following terms.

(a) Spreadsheet: _____

_____

(b) e-mail: _____

_____

11 Tick the boxes (✔) to indicate **true** or **false**.

	True	False
(a) Bebo and Facebook are social networking sites.		
(b) A firewall is an example of computer hardware.		
(c) Twitter is a short form of blog.		
(d) e-mail is a confidential written form of communication.		
(e) A virus is a software program that can infect a computer.		

12 Explain the following terms.

(a) Database: _____

_____

(b) Internet: _____

_____

(c) Computer graphics: _____

_____

13 **(a)** List three costs to a business associated with using computers and having Internet access, other than the cost of the computer itself.

(i) _____

(ii) _____

(iii) _____

(b) List three uses of information technology in a business.

(i) _____

(ii) _____

(iii) _____

(c) List four questions that should be asked before buying a computer.

(i) _____

(ii) _____

(iii) _____

(iv) _____

14 **(a)** Name three sources of finance that a business could use to buy computer equipment costing €12,500. Explain each source of finance.

(i) _____

_____

(ii) _____

_____

(iii) _____

_____

(b) Identify three benefits to a business of using computers.

(i) _____

(ii) _____

(iii) _____

15 **(a)** List two advantages and two disadvantages of using e-mail.

Advantages: **(i)** _____

(ii) _____

Disadvantages: **(i)** _____

(ii) _____

(b) Explain three benefits of using the Internet to either a business or an individual.

(i) _____

(ii) _____

(iii) _____

16 Your school is preparing to buy computer equipment and software costing €20,000.

(a) List four items of hardware that you believe would be necessary.

(i) _____

(ii) _____

(iii) _____

(iv) _____

(b) List three software programs that would be beneficial to the school and education.

(i) _____

(ii) _____

(iii) _____

(c) Identify two possible sources of finance that the school could use to pay for the purchase. Explain each source.

(i) _____

_____

(ii) _____

_____

(d) State three ways in which the school could benefit from buying the computer system.

(i) _____

(ii) _____

(iii) _____

17 In relation to computers and information technology, explain the following terms.

(a) Virus: _____

_____

(b) Menu: _____

_____

(c) Mouse: _____

_____

(d) PC: _____

_____

(e) Search engine: _____

_____

(f) Broadband: _____

_____

(g) Podcast: _____

_____

18 Write a business letter or a report to the owner of a local business setting out the following:

(a) the costs (at least three) associated with operating a computer system;
(b) three ways in which the computer system might affect the business; and
(c) three possible uses of computer technology in the business.

Cash Book and Ledger 1

1 List four reasons why a business should keep accurate records of all of its transactions.

(a) Have record of how much money's been spent

(b) How much money's recieved

(c) See if moneys owed from or to the business

(d) to have an up to date balance sheet.

2 Distinguish between the following terms.

(a) Debit side and credit side: _____

Debit side is the recieving side and
Credit side is the giving.

(b) Trading goods and non-trading goods: Trading goods are goods bought
for resale by a business non trading goods are
goods for by a business for its own use.

3 How would the following transaction be recorded in your business ledger?
Bought goods for resale by cash, €640

Debit _____ account.   Credit €640 —Cash _____ account.

4 How would the following transaction be recorded in your business ledger?
Paid advertising by cheque, €3,250

Debit Advertising _____ account.   Credit €3250 — ~~Advertising~~ Bank _____ account.

5 How would the following transaction be recorded in your business ledger?
Paid office expenses by cash, €160

Debit Office ~~goods~~ expenses _____ account.   Credit €160 ~~Bank~~ Cash _____ account.

6 How would the following transaction be recorded in your business ledger?
Sold trading goods and received a cheque, €1,460

Debit €1460 Bank _____ account.   Credit Sales _____ account.

7 How would the following transaction be recorded in your business ledger?
Bought office equipment by cheque, €2,800

Debit Office equipment _____ account.   Credit €2800 Bank _____ account.

8 How would the following transaction be recorded in your business ledger?
Paid rent by cheque (no. 1), €4,500

Debit ___*rent*___ account.   Credit ___*Bank*___ account.

9 How would the following transaction be recorded in your business ledger?
Received a cheque for rent of a warehouse, €6,600

Debit ___*Bank*___ account.   Credit ___*Warehouse rent*___ account.

10 Record the following transaction in the appropriate ledger accounts.
15 May 2012: sold goods for cash, €340

Debit ___*~~Sales~~ Cash*___ account.   Credit ___*Sales*___ account.

Dr   Cr

Date	Details	F	Total €	Date	Details	F	Total €
				Sales A/C			
				15 May	*Cash*		*340*
				Cash A/C			
15 May	*Sales*		*340*				

11 Record the following transaction in the appropriate ledger accounts.
23 October 2012: purchased goods for resale by cheque, €2,100

Debit ___*Bank ~~a/c~~*___ account.   Credit ___*Purchases a/c*___ account.

Dr   Cr

Date	Details	F	Total €	Date	Details	F	Total €
				Purchases A/C			
				23-Oct	*goods*		*2100*
				Bank A/C			
23-Oct	*Cheque*		*2100*				

12 Record the following transaction in the appropriate ledger accounts.
3 April 2012: paid insurance by cheque, €1,640

Debit _____ account.   Credit _____ account.

Dr   Cr

Date	Details	F	Total €	Date	Details	F	Total €
				Insurance A/C			
3-Apr	*Insurance*		*1640*				
				Bank A/C			
				3-Apr	*Cheque*		*1640*

13 Record the following transaction in the appropriate ledger accounts.
18 January 2013: paid expenses by cash, €165

Debit _____ account.   Credit _____ account.

Dr   Cr

Date	Details	F	Total €	Date	Details	F	Total €
				Expenses A/C			
18 Jan	Cash		165				
				Cash A/C			
				18 Jan	expenses		165

14 Record the following transaction in the appropriate ledger accounts.
29 March 2013: paid wages by cheque (no. 45), €2,820

15 Record the following transaction in the appropriate ledger accounts.
14 September 2013: sold goods, money lodged, €5,760

16 Record the following transaction in the appropriate ledger accounts.
28 November 2013: capital lodged by shareholders, €75,000

17 Record the following transaction in the appropriate ledger accounts.
2 June 2013: bought office computer by cheque (no. 15), €1,250

18 Balance the following bank account at the end of the month.

Dr   Bank Account   Cr

Date	Details	F	Total €	Date	Details	F	Total €
1 Feb	Balance	b/d	1,560	6 Feb	Purchases	GL	1,800
11 Feb	Sales	GL	3,100	17 Feb	Wages	GL	2,400
21 Feb	Sales	GL	3,740	23 Feb	Purchases	GL	1,550
			84	28 Feb	Balance c/d		2650
Mar 1	B		84,00				8460
Mar 1	Balance b/d		2650				

19 Balance the following bank account at the end of the month.

Dr   Bank Account   Cr

Date	Details	F	Total €	Date	Details	F	Total €
1 March	Balance	b/d	5,340	4 March	Wages	GL	1,980
10 March	Sales	GL	2,760	8 March	Purchases	GL	1,830
22 March	Sales	GL	3,555	14 March	Expenses	GL	375
				21 March	Purchases	GL	1,710
				31 Mar	Balance c/d		5760
			11655				11655
1 Apr	Balance b/d		5760				

20 Balance the following bank account at the end of the month.

Dr Bank Account Cr

Date	Details	F	Total €	Date	Details	F	Total €
1 April	Balance	b/d	860	3 April	Purchases	GL	1,100
10 April	Sales	GL	1,670	10 April	Rent	GL	800
17 April	Sales	GL	1,820	18 April	Wages	GL	1,600
24 April	Sales	GL	2,230	23 April	Purchases	GL	1,320

21 Balance the following bank account at the end of the month.

Dr Bank Account Cr

Date	Details	F	Total €	Date	Details	F	Total €
1 May	Balance	b/d	2,640	5 May	Purchases	GL	2,450
16 May	Sales	GL	4,140	16 May	Wages	GL	2,800
				24 May	Insurance	GL	3,300
31 May	Balance c/d		1770				
			8550				8550
				1 June	Balance B/d		1770

Explain the closing balance: _____

22 Balance the following bank account at the end of the month (continuous layout).

Bank Account

Date 2013	Details	F	Dr (€)	Cr (€)	Balance €
1 June	Balance	b/d			7,350
4 June	Purchases	GL		1,800	
10 June	Sales	GL	3,700		
16 June	Wages	GL		2,100	
24 June	Sales	GL	4,050		
25 June	Rent	GL		1,200	
28 June	Advertising	GL		800	

Record the following transactions in the appropriate ledger accounts and balance the accounts on the last date (current year).

23
3 Jan	Sold goods and lodged money	€3,800
4 Jan	Purchased goods for resale by cheque no. 1	€2,125
6 Jan	Sold goods and lodged money	€3,400
7 Jan	Paid wages by cheque no. 2	€2,600

24
12 March	Sold goods and received a cheque	€5,200
13 March	Paid for advertising by cheque no. 1	€1,700
14 March	Sold goods and lodged money	€4,900
15 March	Bought goods and paid by cheque no. 2	€2,600
16 March	Paid wages by cheque no. 3	€3,200

25	1 April	Sold goods and lodged money	€6,000
	2 April	Purchased goods for resale by cheque no. 1	€2,800
	3 April	Bought office furniture by cheque no. 2	€900
	4 April	Sold goods and lodged money	€2,800
	5 April	Paid rent by cheque no. 3	€2,000

26	1 July	Invested €50,000 capital into the business bank account	
	1 July	Bought goods by cheque no. 1	€3,500
	2 July	Bought equipment for business use by cheque no. 2	€6,750
	3 July	Paid insurance by cheque no. 3	€2,200
	4 July	Paid wages by cheque no. 4	€2,400
	5 July	Sold goods and lodged money	€1,400

27	1 Aug	Sold goods and lodged money	€2,900
	2 Aug	Bought goods for resale by cheque no. 11	€2,100
	3 Aug	Sold goods and lodged money	€2,600
	3 Aug	Paid expenses by cheque no. 12	€550
	4 Aug	Paid electricity by cheque no. 13	€730
	5 Aug	Cash sales	€850

Record the following transactions in the cash book and the appropriate ledger accounts, balance the accounts and extract a trial balance on the last date (current year).

28	2 Jan	Commenced business with capital lodged	€75,000
	3 Jan	Bought goods for resale by cheque no. 1	€12,000
	3 Jan	Paid insurance by cheque no. 2	€6,200
	4 Jan	Bought office furniture by cheque no. 3	€8,400
	4 Jan	Bought office computer equipment by cheque no. 4	€2,800
	5 Jan	Sold goods and lodged money	€4,200
	6 Jan	Paid wages by cheque no. 5	€1,800

29	9 Jan	Sold goods and lodged money	€5,800
	9 Jan	Paid rent by cheque no. 6	€3,200
	10 Jan	Paid electricity by cheque no. 7	€710
	11 Jan	Sold goods and lodged money	€2,100
	12 Jan	Paid for advertising by cheque no. 8	€2,800
	13 Jan	Sold goods and lodged money	€2,400
	13 Jan	Paid wages by cheque no. 9	€1,800
	13 Jan	Paid expenses by cheque no. 10	€350

30	1 March	Cash sales	€720
	2 March	Paid expenses by cash	€240
	3 March	Sold goods and lodged money	€3,700
	3 March	Bought goods for resale by cheque no. 1	€1,800
	4 March	Paid rent by cheque no. 2	€1,200
	5 March	Sold goods and lodged money	€3,450
	5 March	Paid wages by cheque no. 3	€2,100
	5 March	Paid telephone bill by cheque no. 4	€300

31

1 May	Commenced business with capital, lodged	€100,000
1 May	Bought office furniture by cheque no. 1	€6,500
1 May	Bought equipment by cheque no. 2	€15,000
2 May	Bought goods for resale by cheque no. 3	€18,000
3 May	Paid rent by cheque no. 4	€2,500
4 May	Paid electricity by cheque no. 5	€500
5 May	Sold goods and lodged money	€4,300
5 May	Paid wages by cheque no. 6	€2,400

32

1 March	Commenced business with capital, lodged	€70,000
1 March	Paid rent by cheque no. 1	€1,800
2 March	Bought goods for resale by cheque no. 2	€8,700
2 March	Bought office equipment by cheque no. 3	€4,500
3 March	Paid insurance by cheque no. 4	€4,000
4 March	Paid telephone by cheque no. 5	€400
5 March	Sold goods and lodged money	€2,900
5 March	Paid wages by cheque no. 6	€1,800

33

1 Sept	Sold goods and lodged money	€4,900
1 Sept	Paid for advertising by cheque no. 6	€2,200
2 Sept	Purchased goods for resale by cheque no. 7	€2,500
3 Sept	Cash sales, lodged	€3,800
3 Sept	Bought an office desk by cheque no. 8	€550
4 Sept	Cash sales, lodged	€1,600
4 Sept	Withdrew cash from the bank	€600
4 Sept	Paid office expenses by cash	€350
5 Sept	Cash sales, lodged	€1,800
5 Sept	Paid wages by cheque no. 9	€2,600

34

1 Oct	Commenced business with capital, lodged	€25,000
1 Oct	Paid rent by cheque no. 1	€1,250
1 Oct	Withdrew cash from the bank	€1,000
2 Oct	Paid expenses by cash	€400
3 Oct	Bought goods by cheque no. 2	€7,200
4 Oct	Cash sales	€1,100
4 Oct	Paid insurance by cheque no. 3	€2,400
5 Oct	Cash sales	€1,600
5 Oct	Paid wages by cheque no. 4	€1,500
5 Oct	Lodged cash to bank	€2,300

35

1 Nov	Cash sales, lodged	€2,200
1 Nov	Paid advertising by cheque no. 1	€1,300
2 Nov	Cash sales, lodged	€2,000
2 Nov	Withdrew cash from bank	€500
3 Nov	Cash sales, lodged	€1,800
3 Nov	Paid rent by cheque no. 2	€1,600
4 Nov	Cash sales, lodged	€2,300
4 Nov	Paid office expenses by cash	€340
5 Nov	Cash sales, lodged	€2,500
5 Nov	Bought goods for resale by cheque no. 3	€3,200
5 Nov	Paid wages by cheque no. 4	€2,200

36 Convert the following account from a T-shaped account to a continuous presentation, and balance **both** accounts (current year).

Dr   Bank Account   Cr

Date	Details	F	Total €	Date	Details	F	Total €
1 Feb	Balance	b/d	5,700	11 Feb	Purchases	GL1	5,600
9 Feb	Sales	GL2	4,800	15 Feb	Rent	GL3	2,500
16 Feb	Sales	GL2	5,300	24 Feb	Wages	GL4	4,800
23 Feb	Sales	GL2	5,650				

37 Convert the following account from a continuous presentation to a T-shaped account, and balance **both** accounts (current year).

Bank Account

Date	Details	F	Dr (€)	Cr (€)	Balance
1 July	Balance	b/d			12,360
3 July	Purchases	GL		4,800	
13 July	Sales	GL	7,450		
18 July	Wages	GL		5,400	
21 July	Rent	GL		1,800	
25 July	Sales	GL	7,800		
27 July	Insurance	GL		3,100	
29 July	Expenses	GL		300	

38 The following account appeared in the ledger of Roberts Ltd.

Dr   Bank Account   Cr

Date	Details	F	Total €	Date	Details	F	Total €
1 Jan	Balance	b/d	15,680	3 Jan	Purchases	GL	4,300
4 Jan	Sales	GL	7,800	5 Jan	Wages	GL	2,200

Balance the account and complete the following sentences to explain the entries.

On 1 January, Roberts Ltd _____

On 3 January, Roberts Ltd _____

On 4 January, Roberts Ltd _____

On 5 January, Roberts Ltd _____

39 The following account appeared in the ledger of Thompson Ltd.

Dr   Equipment Account   Cr

Date	Details	F	Total €	Date	Details	F	Total €
1 Jan	Balance	b/d	38,000				
28 Jan	Bank	CB	10,500				

Balance the account and complete the following sentences to explain the entries.

On 1 January, Thompson Ltd _____

_____

On 28 January, Thompson Ltd _____

_____

40 The following entries appeared in the bank columns of Mayo Ltd's cash book.

Dr   Cash Book   Cr

Date	Details	F	Bank €	Date	Details	F	Bank €
4 March	Sales	GL	5,300	1 March	Balance	b/d	6,700

Balance the account and complete the following sentences to explain the entries.

On 1 March, Mayo Ltd _____

_____

On 4 March, Mayo Ltd _____

_____

Cash Book and Ledger 2

1 Explain the following terms.

(a) Debtors: _____

_____

(b) Creditors: _____

_____

(c) Analysed cash book: _____

_____

2 Study the analysed cash book on page 246 of the textbook and answer the following questions.

(a) How much in total did the business spend on expenses? _____

(b) How much in total did the business receive from sales? _____

(c) How much did the business spend on electricity? _____

(d) How much is left in the business bank account at the end of the month? _____

Record the following transactions in the analysed cash book, post to the ledger and extract a trial balance on the final date (current year).
Analysis columns: Debit (Dr) side – Cash, Bank, Sales.
**   Credit (Cr) side – Cash, Bank, Purchases, Creditors, Expenses.**

3
1 March	Cash sales, lodged	€4,600
1 March	Paid rent by cheque no. 11	€1,700
2 March	Cash sales	€1,150
3 March	Bought goods by cheque no. 12	€2,200
4 March	Cash sales, lodged	€2,820
5 March	Paid expenses by cash	€370
5 March	Paid wages by cheque no. 13	€1,950

4
1 June	Cash sales	€800
2 June	Bought office supplies by cash	€380
2 June	Cash sales, lodged	€1,350
2 June	Paid advertising by cheque no. 1	€1,000
3 June	Cash sales, lodged	€1,620
3 June	Paid office expenses by cash	€140
4 June	Bought goods for resale by cheque no. 2	€1,720
5 June	Cash sales, lodged	€2,800
5 June	Paid wages by cheque no. 3	€2,500

5	1 Oct	Lodged €40,000 capital into the business bank account	
	1 Oct	Bought goods for resale by cheque no. 1	€12,800
	2 Oct	Bought equipment for business use by cheque no. 2	€9,600
	3 Oct	Paid rent by cheque no. 3	€1,600
	3 Oct	Paid insurance by cheque no. 4	€3,700
	5 Oct	Cash sales, lodged	€2,100
	5 Oct	Paid wages by cheque no. 5	€2,800

6	1 Nov	Cash sales, lodged	€5,300
	1 Nov	Paid advertising by cheque no. 1	€2,500
	2 Nov	Cash sales, lodged	€4,400
	2 Nov	Bought goods for resale by cheque no. 2	€3,600
	3 Nov	Paid rent by cheque by no. 3	€1,400
	4 Nov	Cash sales, lodged	€5,100
	5 Nov	Paid Troy Ltd, a creditor, by cheque no. 4	€3,000
	5 Nov	Paid wages by cheque no. 5	€2,400

7	1 Feb	Cash sales, lodged	€7,000
	1 Feb	Paid insurance by cheque no. 1	€2,400
	2 Feb	Cash sales, lodged	€5,300
	2 Feb	Paid electricity by cheque no. 2	€420
	3 Feb	Paid Ryan Ltd, a creditor, by cheque no. 3	€4,280
	4 Feb	Cash sales, lodged	€7,300
	4 Feb	Withdrew cash from bank	€1,000
	4 Feb	Paid office expenses by cash	€300
	5 Feb	Cash sales, lodged	€5,900
	5 Feb	Paid wages by cheque no. 4	€6,800
	5 Feb	Paid rent by cheque no. 5	€2,100

8	1 May	Cash sales, lodged	€2,400
	1 May	Paid expenses by cheque no. 11	€800
	2 May	Cash sales, lodged	€2,100
	2 May	Purchased goods for resale by cheque no. 12	€3,000
	3 May	Cash sales, lodged	€1,900
	3 May	Withdrew cash from bank	€500
	3 May	Paid office expenses by cash	€200
	4 May	Cash sales, lodged	€2,000
	4 May	Paid rent by cheque no. 13	€1,600
	5 May	Cash sales, lodged	€2,300
	5 May	Bought office stationery by cash	€100
	5 May	Paid wages by cheque no. 14	€2,800

9	1 Aug	Commenced business with €75,000 capital in the business bank account	
	1 Aug	Bought equipment for business use by cheque no. 1	€9,000
	1 Aug	Purchased goods for resale by cheque no. 2	€12,200
	1 Aug	Bought office furniture by cheque no. 3	€6,400
	2 Aug	Paid rent by cheque no. 4	€1,750
	3 Aug	Paid insurance by cheque no. 5	€2,800
	3 Aug	Cash sales, lodged	€1,600
	4 Aug	Paid expenses by cheque no. 6	€450
	5 Aug	Paid wages by cheque no. 7	€5,400
	5 Aug	Cash sales, lodged	€1,900

10 Complete the following.

(a) VAT stands for _____

(b) VAT is a tax on _____

(c) The current rates of VAT are: _____%; _____%; _____%; and _____%.

(d) What does a retailer registered to collect VAT have to do? _____

_____

_____

11 A computer system is quoted as €5,600 (excl. VAT @ 21%). Calculate the total price including VAT.

_____

12 A building contractor quotes €80,000 (excl. VAT @ 13.5%). Calculate the cost including VAT.

_____

13 A television costs €840 (excl. VAT @21%). Calculate the cost including VAT.

_____

14 A computer costs €500 (excl. VAT @ 21%). Calculate the cost including VAT.

_____

15 Find the total cost, including VAT, of each of the following.

(a) €120 excl. VAT @ 21.5%	**(b)** €7,200 excl. VAT @ 13.5%	**(c)** €900 excl. VAT @ 21.5%

16 Calculate the original cost, excluding VAT, of each of the following.

(a) €729 incl. VAT @ 21.5%	**(b)** €5,902 incl. VAT @ 13.5%	**(c)** €558.90 incl. VAT @ 21.5%

17 Calculate the original cost, excluding VAT, of each of the following.

(a) €272.40 incl. VAT @ 13.5%

(b) €18,160 incl. VAT @ 13.5%

(c) €2,187, incl. VAT @ 21.5%

18 The following VAT a/c appeared in the ledger of Roper Ltd.

Dr   Vat A/C   Cr

Date	Details	F	Total €	Date	Details	F	Total €
31 March	Purchases	CB	1,720	31 March	Sales	CB	3,655
31 March	Balance	c/d	1,935				
			3,655				3,655
				31 March	Balance	b/d	1,935

Explain **each** of the above transactions for Roper Ltd.

31 March purchases: _____

_____

31 March sales: _____

_____

31 March balance b/d: _____

_____

19 List three steps that a business can take to monitor and/or reduce overheads.

(a) _____

(b) _____

(c) _____

Record the following transactions in the analysed cash book, post to the ledger and extract a trial balance on the final date (current year).
Analysis columns: Debit (Dr) side – Bank, Sales, VAT, Debtors.
**   Credit (Cr) side – Bank, Purchases, VAT, Creditors, Expenses.**

20

1 Feb	Shareholders lodged €150,000 into the business bank account	
2 Feb	Purchased goods for resale by cheque no. 1	€14,000
2 Feb	Purchased furniture for business use by cheque no. 2	€8,800
3 Feb	Paid insurance by cheque no. 3	€4,750
3 Feb	Paid for advertising by cheque no. 4	€7,500
4 Feb	Cash sales, lodged	€1,600
4 Feb	Paid rent by cheque no. 5	€2,000
5 Feb	Cash sales, lodged	€2,200
5 Feb	Paid wages by cheque no. 6	€3,600
	(excluding 21% VAT on purchases and sales of trading goods)	

21

1 March	Cash sales, lodged	€14,000
1 March	Purchased goods for resale by cheque no. 1	€6,000
2 March	Paid for advertising by cheque no. 2	€4,600
2 March	Paid electricity bill by cheque no. 3	€750
3 March	Cash sales, lodged	€12,000
3 March	Purchased equipment for business use by cheque no. 4	€5,800
4 March	Purchased goods for resale by cheque no. 5	€4,000
5 March	Cash sales, lodged	€15,000
5 March	Paid a creditor, Topaz Ltd, by cheque no. 6 (full settlement)	€6,200
5 March	Paid wages by cheque no. 7	€4,800
	(excluding 21% VAT on purchases and sales of trading goods)	

22

1 April	Cash sales, lodged	€8,000
1 April	Purchased goods for resale by cheque no. 1	€3,600
2 April	Paid for insurance by cheque no. 2	€2,600
3 April	Cash sales, lodged	€7,000
3 April	Purchased office furniture by cheque no. 3	€2,400
4 April	Purchased goods for resale by cheque no. 4	€3,000
5 April	Cash sales, lodged	€7,200
5 April	Paid expenses by cheque no. 5	€800
5 April	Paid wages by cheque no. 6	€4,500
	(excluding 13.5% VAT on purchases and sales of trading goods)	

23

8 May	Cash sales, lodged	€6,000
8 May	Paid expenses by cheque no. 1	€500
9 May	Purchased goods for resale by cheque no. 2	€4,000
10 May	Cash sales, lodged	€5,000
11 May	Paid rent by cheque no. 3	€1,400
11 May	A debtor, Brouder Ltd, paid a cheque in full settlement	€2,200
12 May	Cash sales, lodged	€7,000
12 May	Paid wages by cheque no. 4	€3,800
12 May	Purchased goods for resale by cheque no. 3	€3,000
	(excluding 21% VAT on purchases and sales of trading goods)	

24 Record the following transactions for the month of July (current year). Post the relevant entries to the ledger and extract a trial balance.

Analysis columns: Debit (Dr) side – Bank, Sales, VAT, Debtors.
Credit (Cr) side – Bank, Purchases, VAT, Creditors, Expenses.

3 July	Cash sales, lodged	€34,050 (€30,000 + €4,050 VAT)
6 July	Purchases for resale, cheque no. 1	€14,000 + VAT @13.5%
12 July	Paid wages by cheque no. 2	€10,400
18 July	Cash sales, lodged	€47,670 (€42,000 + €5,670 VAT)
20 July	Paid advertising by cheque no. 3	€8,000
24 July	Purchases for resale, cheque no. 4	€22,000 + VAT @13.5%
28 July	Paid rent by cheque no. 5	€4,500

25 Record the following transactions for the month of July (current year). Post the relevant entries to the ledger and extract a trial balance.

Analysis columns: Debit (Dr) side – Bank, Sales, VAT, Debtors.
Credit (Cr) side – Bank, Purchases, VAT, Creditors, Expenses.

1 July	Shareholders invest capital €200,000 and this was lodged	
3 July	Purchases for resale by cheque no. 1	€40,000 + VAT @21.5%
4 July	Paid lease by cheque no. 2	€10,000
14 July	Cash sales, lodged	€24,300 (€20,000 + €4,300 VAT)
20 July	Paid wages by cheque no. 3	€9,200
21 July	Purchases for resale by cheque no. 4	€32,000 + VAT @ 21.5%
22 July	Paid insurance by cheque no. 5	€7,500
25 July	Paid Ledl Ltd, a creditor, by cheque no. 6	€6,000 (in full settlement)
28 July	Cash sales, lodged	€48,600 (€40,000 + €8,600 VAT)

26 Record the following transactions for the month of August 2012. Post the relevant entries to the ledger and extract a trial balance.

Analysis columns: Debit (Dr) side Bank, Sales, VAT, Debtors.
Credit (Cr) side – Bank, Purchases, VAT, Creditors, Expenses.

2 Aug	Cash sales, lodged	€48,600 (€40,000 + €8,600 VAT)
7 Aug	Purchases for resale by cheque no. 6	€30,000 + VAT @21.5%
12 Aug	Paid wages by cheque no. 7	€4,500
16 Aug	Cash sales, lodged	€63,180 (€52,000 + €11,180 VAT)
18 Aug	Paid advertising by cheque no. 8	€11,500
21 Aug	Paid Thomond Ltd, a creditor, by cheque no. 9	€7,500
22 Aug	Purchases for resale by cheque no. 10	€28,000 + VAT @21.5%
24 Aug	A debtor, Roberts Ltd, paid €2,500 on account and this was lodged (receipt no. 23)	
28 Aug	Cash sales, lodged	€54,675 (€45,000 + €9,675 VAT)

Bank Reconciliation Statement

1 Explain the following terms.

(a) Bank statement: _____

_____

(b) Bank charges: _____

_____

(c) Bank reconciliation statement: _____

_____

2 Give three reasons why a bank statement might differ from the bank account in the cash book.

(a) _____

(b) _____

(c) _____

3

BANK OF IRELAND

Eyre Square, Galway.

Branch Code: 54 88 26

Ms Jane Sweeney
Renmore
Co. Galway

Account Name: Jane Sweeney
Account No.: 12345769
Date: 28 June 2011

Bank Statement 28 June 2011

Date	Particulars	Debit €	Credit €	Balance €
June				
1	Balance			820
14	Paypath		2,200	3,020
15	Cheque no. 13	180		2,840
20	Cheque no. 14	520		2,320
27	Cheque no. 15	195		2,125
27	ATM Mallow	300		1,825

Dr   Cash Book (Bank Account)   **Cr**

Date 2011	Details	Bank €	Date 2011	Details	Cheque no.	Bank €
June			June			
1	Balance b/d	820	9	Groceries	13	180
14	Paypath	2,200	17	Insurance	14	520
			23	Groceries	15	195
			27	Car repairs	16	220
			30	Balance c/d		1,905
		3,020				3,020
1 July	Balance b/d	1,905				

Prepare the following.
(a) The adjusted cash book.
(b) The bank reconciliation statement.
(c) Explain the following terms: **(i)** paypath; **(ii)** ATM.

4

Bank Statement 29 March 2011

Date	Particulars	Debit €	Credit €	Balance €
March				
1	Balance			1,420
4	Cheque no. 9	250		1,170
10	ATM Athlone	200		970
14	S/O	350		620
21	Paypath		2,500	3,120
23	Cheque no. 11	500		2,620
27	Bank charges	20		2,600

Dr   Cash Book (Bank Account)   **Cr**

Date 2011	Details	Bank €	Date 2011	Details	Cheque no.	Bank €
March			March			
1	Balance b/d	1,420	2	Shopping	9	250
21	Salary	2,500	10	ATM cash		200
			16	Car tax	10	220
			21	Insurance	11	500
			31	Balance c/d		2,750
		3,920				3,920
1 April	Balance b/d	2,750				

Prepare the following.
(a) The adjusted cash book.
(b) The bank reconciliation statement.
(c) Explain the following terms: **(i)** S/O; **(ii)** Bank charges.

5

Bank Statement 28 November 2011

Date	Particulars	Debit €	Credit €	Balance €
Nov				
1	Balance			2,800
7	Insurance S/O	168		2,632
11	Cheque no. 20	840		1,792
21	Cheque no. 21	180		1,612
26	Cheque no. 23	560		1,052
27	Paypath		2,100	3,152

Dr   **Cash Book (Bank Account)**   **Cr**

Date 2011	Details	Bank €	Date 2011	Details	Cheque no.	Bank €
Nov			Nov			
1	Balance b/d	2,800	8	Health insurance	20	840
27	Salary	2,100	17	Groceries	21	180
29	Lodgement	140	21	Clothes	22	84
			23	Heating oil	23	560
			27	Groceries	24	156
			30	Balance c/d		3,220
		5,040				5,040
1 Dec	Balance b/d	3,220				

Prepare the following.

(a) The adjusted cash book.

(b) The bank reconciliation statement.

(c) Give one reason why the lodgement of €140 does not appear in the bank statement. _____

_____

6

Bank Statement 29 August 2011

Date	Particulars	Debit €	Credit €	Balance €
Aug				
1	Balance			800
10	Cheque no. 6	195		605
15	Salary (Paypath)		1,800	2,405
21	ATM Limerick	150		2,255
28	Mortgage S/O	850		1,405

Dr   **Cash Book (Bank Account)**   **Cr**

Date 2011	Details	Bank €	Date 2011	Details	Cheque no.	Bank €
August			August			
1	Balance b/d	800	6	Tesco	6	195
15	Salary	1,800	21	ATM cash		150
29	Lodgement (lotto)	150	27	Tesco	7	220
			30	Balance c/d		2,185
		2,750				2,750
1 Sept	Balance b/d	2,185				

Prepare the following.
(a) The adjusted cash book.
(b) The bank reconciliation statement.
(c) Explain why the dates between the two documents do not always correspond.

7 Explain the following terms.

(a) Direct debit: _____

_____

(b) Credit transfer: _____

_____

(c) Interest payment: _____

_____

(d) Bank overdraft: _____

_____

8 Distinguish between the following terms.

(a) Standing order and direct debit: _____

_____

_____

(b) Bank statement and bank reconciliation statement: _____

_____

_____

_____

9

Bank Statement 29 March 2011

Date	Particulars	Debit €	Credit €	Balance €
March				
1	Balance			672
3	ATM, Athy	240		432
6	Cheque no. 4	608		176 Dr
10	Paypath		2,880	2,704
17	ATM, Athy	320		2,384
21	Insurance S/O	150		2,234
24	Cheque no. 6	185		2,049
25	Lodgement		160	2,209
28	Interest	5		2,204

Dr   **Cash Book (Bank Account)**   **Cr**

Date 2011	Details	Bank €	Date 2011	Details	Cheque no.	Bank €
March			March			
1	Balance b/d	672	3	ATM cash		240
10	Salary	2,880	4	Furniture sales	4	608
25	Lodgement	160	17	ATM cash		320
			19	Spar – groceries	5	165
			21	Clothes	6	185
			31	Balance c/d		2,194
		3,712				3,712
1 April	Balance b/d	2,194				

Prepare the following.
(a) The adjusted cash book.
(b) The bank reconciliation statement.
(c) Explain what is meant by '176 Dr' on the bank statement on 6 March: _____

_____

(d) Why does interest appear on the bank statement? _____

_____

(e) Explain the term 'Insurance S/O': _____

_____

10

Bank Statement 29 July 2011

Date	Particulars	Debit €	Credit €	Balance €
July				
1	Balance			240 Dr
3	Lodgement		1,600	1,360
8	Cheque no. 15	420		940
10	ATM Cobh	250		690
19	Lodgement		500	1,190
20	Cheque no. 17	400		790
23	Cheque no. 16	270		520
28	Charges & interest	10		510

Cash Book (Bank Account)

Dr — Cr

Date 2011	Details	Bank €	Date 2011	Details	Cheque no.	Bank €
July			July			
3	Salary	1,600	1	Balance b/d		240
19	Overtime	500	3	Repairs	14	60
28	Lodgement	300	5	Insurance	15	420
			10	ATM cash		250
			15	Tesco	16	270
			17	Car tax	17	400
			31	Balance c/d		760
		2,400				2,400
1 Aug	Balance b/d	760				

Prepare the following.
(a) The adjusted cash book.
(b) The bank reconciliation statement.

11

Bank Statement 29 January 2011

Date	Particulars	Debit €	Credit €	Balance €
Jan 2011				
1	Balance			450 Dr
4	Paypath		1,650	1,200
6	Mortgage S/O	930		270
8	Cheque no. 1	185		85
8	ATM Limerick	240		155 Dr
12	DD Meteor	85		240 Dr
19	Paypath		1,650	1,410
22	Cheque no. 2	240		1,170
23	ATM Limerick	180		990
28	Interest & fees	15		975

Dr   Cash Book (Bank Account)   Cr

Date 2011	Details	Bank €	Date 2011	Details	Cheque no.	Bank €
Jan			Jan			
4	Salary	1,650	1	Balance b/d		450
19	Salary	1,650	6	Mortgage		930
29	Tax refund	320	7	Groceries		185
			8	ATM cash	1	240
			19	Groceries		240
			23	ATM cash	2	180
			27	Clothes		160
			31	Balance c/d		1,235
		3,620				3,620
1 Feb	Balance b/d	1,235				

Prepare the following.
(a) The adjusted cash book.
(b) The bank reconciliation statement.
(c) Explain the term Paypath, and give one benefit of using it for the employer and one different benefit for the employee.

_____

_____

Employer benefit: _____

_____

Employee benefit: _____

_____

12

Bank Statement 29 August 2011

Date	Particulars	Debit €	Credit €	Balance €
Aug 2011				
1	Balance			400
12	Paypath		2,500	2,900
14	Cheque no. 1	300		2,600
16	Cheque no. 3	750		1,850
21	ATM Dundalk	400		1,450
25	ESB DD	190		1,260
28	Bank charges	16		1,244

Dr   **Cash Book (Bank Account)**   **Cr**

Date 2011	Details	Bank €	Date 2011	Details	Cheque no.	Bank €
Aug			Aug			
1	Balance b/d	400	10	Furniture	1	300
12	Salary	2,500	11	Petrol	2	70
25	Lodgement	150	14	Car insurance	3	750
			19	Car repairs	4	380
			21	ATM cash		400
			24	Superquinn	5	220
31	Balance c/d	50	27	Holiday	6	980
		3,100				3,100
			1 Sept	Balance b/d		50

Prepare the following.

(a) The adjusted cash book.

(b) The bank reconciliation statement.

(c) Explain the bank balance in the cash book on 1 September 2011.

(d) Explain the adjusted bank balance of 1 September 2011.

13 Anna Kovak opened a current account in the Bank of Ireland on 1 October 2011 and lodged €500. The following are her transactions for the month of October:

2011		
2 Oct	Purchased groceries, cheque no. 1	€90
5 Oct	Withdrew by ATM	€150
11 Oct	Lodged	€800
12 Oct	Purchased petrol by cheque no. 2	€80
14 Oct	Purchased clothes by cheque no. 3	€210
16 Oct	Purchased groceries by cheque no. 4	€95
20 Oct	Withdrew by ATM	€150
24 Oct	Purchased cosmetics by cheque no. 5	€70
28 Oct	Lodged	€750

(a) Write up Anna's own records (cash book) of her bank transactions for the month of October.

(b) Compare Anna's own records with the bank statement she received (next page). Make whatever adjustments are necessary to Anna's own records and then prepare a bank reconciliation statement.

Bank Statement 29 October 2011

Date	Particulars	Debit €	Credit €	Balance €
Oct 2011				
1	Lodgement			500
5	ATM	150		350
7	Cheque no. 1	90		260
11	Lodgement		800	1,060
14	S/O	200		860
16	Cheque no. 3	210		650
17	C/T		200	850
19	Cheque no. 4	95		755
20	ATM	150		605
27	Cheque no. 5	70		535

(c) Give two reasons for preparing a bank reconciliation statement.

(i) _____

(ii) _____

14 Princess Holdings opened a current account in Allied Irish Bank on 1 February 2011 and lodged €25,000. The following transactions took place during February:

2011
3 Feb	Paid insurance by cheque no. 1	€2,800
5 Feb	Bought goods for resale by cheque no. 2	€7,600
8 Feb	Sales, lodged	€4,800
11 Feb	Paid rent by cheque no. 3	€2,100
14 Feb	Paid a creditor, Mirex Ltd, by cheque no. 4	€1,400
16 Feb	Sales, lodged	€5,600
20 Feb	Bought goods for resale by cheque no. 5	€6,700
24 Feb	Sales, lodged	€5,700
27 Feb	Paid electricity by cheque no. 6	€1,200
28 Feb	Bought office equipment by cheque no. 7	€1,100

(a) Prepare Princess Holdings' own records (cash book) of their bank transactions for the month of February.
(b) Compare Princess Holdings' own records with the bank statement that they received (next page). Make whatever adjustments are necessary to Princess Holdings' own records and then prepare a bank reconciliation statement on 28 February 2011.

Bank Statement 26 February 2011

Date	Particulars	Debit €	Credit €	Balance €
Feb 2011				
1	Lodgement			25,000
6	Cheque no. 1	2,800		22,200
8	Lodgement		4,800	27,000
9	Cheque no. 2	7,600		19,400
14	Cheque no. 3	2,100		17,300
16	Lodgement		5,600	22,900
20	Standing order – Paypath	3,400		19,500
23	Cheque no. 5	6,700		12,800
24	Lodgement		5,700	18,500
26	Fees	20		18,480

15 Saunders Ltd opened a current account in Permanent TSB on 1 March 2011 and lodged €30,000. The following transactions took place during March:

2011		
2 March	Paid rent by cheque no. 1	€1,600
3 March	Bought equipment by cheque no. 2	€5,200
4 March	Bought goods for resale by cheque no. 3	€6,200
11 March	Cash sales, lodged	€2,800
12 March	Bought office furniture by cheque no. 4	€1,250
18 March	Cash sales, lodged	€3,400
19 March	Bought goods for resale by cheque no. 5	€5,700
21 March	Paid advertising by cheque no. 6	€4,600
24 March	Paid insurance by cheque no. 7	€2,200
25 March	Cash sales, lodged	€6,300
29 March	Paid expenses by cheque no. 8	€900

(a) Prepare Saunders Ltd's own records (cash book) of their bank transactions for the month of March 2011.

(b) Compare Saunders Ltd's own records with the bank statement that they received (next page). Make whatever adjustments are necessary to Saunders Ltd's own records and then prepare a bank reconciliation statement on 31 March 2011.

Bank Statement 29 March 2011

Date	Particulars	Debit €	Credit €	Balance €
March 2011				
1	Lodgement			30,000
5	Cheque no. 1	1,600		28,400
8	Cheque no. 2	5,200		23,200
11	Lodgement		2,800	26,000
12	Cheque no. 3	6,200		19,800
16	Cheque no. 4	1,250		18,550
18	Lodgement		3,400	21,950
22	Standing order – Paypath	5,200		16,750
23	Cheque no. 5	5,700		11,050
24	Cheque no. 6	4,600		6,450
25	Lodgement		6,300	12,750
27	Credit transfer		5,000	17,750
28	Fees	15		17,735

Petty Cash Book

1 Petra Kovalenko is the petty cashier in the office. Complete the following petty cash vouchers.
   (a) On 4 February 2012 she signed a petty cash voucher (no. 11) for John O'Brien to cover postage of €15.00.
   (b) On 5 February 2012 she signed a petty cash voucher (no. 12) for Anna Roper for office stationery €22.00.

(a)

PETTY CASH VOUCHER	No.: Date:
Details	Amount €
Signature:	
Petty Cashier:	

(b)

PETTY CASH VOUCHER	No.: Date:
Details	Amount €
Signature:	
Petty Cashier:	

2 James O'Connor is the petty cashier in the office. Complete the following petty cash vouchers.
   (a) On 10 March 2012 he signed a petty cash voucher (no. 35) for Conor Ryan to cover a taxi fare of €12.00.
   (b) On 12 March 2012 he signed a petty cash voucher (no. 36) for Tracey Roberts for tea/coffee €8.50.

(a)

PETTY CASH VOUCHER	No.: Date:
Details	Amount €
Signature:	
Petty Cashier:	

(b)

PETTY CASH VOUCHER	No.: Date:
Details	Amount €
Signature:	
Petty Cashier:	

3 Mark O'Keeffe is the petty cashier in the office. Complete the following petty cash vouchers.
   (a) On 20 May 2012 he signed a petty cash voucher (no. 36) for Olivia Cusack to cover parcel post of €7.60.
   (b) On 23 May 2012 he signed a petty cash voucher (no. 37) for Shaun Roberts for ink cartridges €32.00.

(a)

PETTY CASH VOUCHER	No.: Date:
Details	Amount €
Signature:	
Petty Cashier:	

(b)

PETTY CASH VOUCHER	No.: Date:
Details	Amount €
Signature:	
Petty Cashier:	

4   Explain how the imprest system of petty cash works. _____

_____

_____

_____

5   List three advantages of using the petty cash imprest system.

(a) _____

(b) _____

(c) _____

6   Using the petty cash book on page 269 of the textbook, answer the following questions.

(a) How much in total was spent on stationery? _____

(b) How much did the petty cashier receive to restore the imprest? _____

(c) Explain the following terms.

   (i)   Sundries: _____

   _____

   (ii) Imprest: _____

   _____

7   The petty cashier has an imprest of €200 a month. During March 2012, the petty cashier spent €149 out of petty cash. How much will she receive on 1 April 2012 to restore the imprest? Tick (✓) the appropriate box.

(a) €200 ☐   **(b)** €51 ☐   **(c)** €149 ☐   **(d)** €49 ☐

8   The petty cashier has an imprest of €160 a month. During October 2012, the petty cashier spent €118 out of petty cash. How much will he receive on 1 November 2012 to restore the imprest? Tick (✓) the appropriate box.

(a) €42 ☐   **(b)** €118 ☐   **(c)** €202 ☐   **(d)** €160 ☐

9   The petty cashier has an imprest of €240 a month. During May 2012, the petty cashier spent €228 out of petty cash. How much will she receive on 1 June 2012 to restore the imprest? Tick (✓) the appropriate box.

(a) €252 ☐   **(b)** €240 ☐   **(c)** €12 ☐   **(d)** €228 ☐

10 The petty cashier uses a petty cash book to keep an account of small office expenses. He begins each month with an imprest of €250. Here is what happened in July 2012.

July 2012	Details	Voucher no.	€
1	Balance		250.00
2	Bought postage stamps	1	27.50
5	Paid for two reams of paper	2	10.00
9	Paid for office cleaning materials	3	14.00
11	Paid for taxi fare	4	12.50
16	Bought postage stamps	5	11.00
19	Paid for office cleaning	6	40.00
21	Bought office stationery	7	24.00
23	Paid for postage stamps	8	27.50
26	Paid for tea/coffee for the office	9	18.00
27	Paid for repairs to lock	10	25.00

Complete and balance the petty cash book for the month of July, using the following analysis columns: **Postage, Stationery, Cleaning** and **Sundries**, and restore the imprest. Show the posting of the totals of the analysis columns to their accounts in the ledger.

11 The petty cashier uses a petty cash book to keep an account of small office expenses. She begins each month with an imprest of €240. Here is what happened in June 2012.

June 2012	Details	Voucher no.	€
1	Balance		240.00
2	Bought groceries	1	11.50
3	Bought postage stamps	2	16.50
7	Bought stationery	3	30.00
9	Paid for office cleaning materials	4	16.00
12	Paid for courier	5	18.00
16	Bought postage stamps	6	27.50
19	Bought office stationery	7	18.50
21	Paid for postage stamps	8	16.50
24	Paid for tea/coffee for the office	9	18.00
26	Paid for cleaning materials	10	7.60
28	Paid for photocopier repairs	11	30.00
30	Received a cheque to restore the imprest		

(a) Complete and balance the petty cash book for the month of June, using the following analysis columns: **Postage, Stationery, Cleaning, Groceries** and **Sundries**, and restore the imprest. Show the posting of the totals of the analysis columns to their accounts in the ledger.

(b) Complete the petty cash voucher for 24 June submitted by Joan Flannery (Petty cashier: Helen Loftus).

PETTY CASH VOUCHER	No.: Date:
Details	Amount €
Signature:	
Petty Cashier:	

12 The petty cashier uses a petty cash book to keep an account of small office expenses. He begins each month with an imprest of €300. Here is what happened in September 2012.

Sept 2012	Details	Voucher no.	€
1	Balance		300.00
3	Paid for postage	1	27.50
5	Bought envelopes	2	10.00
8	Paid a donation to a charity	3	15.00
9	Bought stationery	4	32.00
11	Paid a fare for a sales representative	5	36.00
12	Paid the office cleaner	6	35.00
15	Paid for postage	7	27.50
16	Paid for repairs to an office printer	8	30.00
18	Paid for parcel post	9	7.50
22	Paid a fare for the sales manager	10	16.00
26	Paid the office cleaner	11	35.00
27	Purchased stationery	12	21.00
30	Received a cheque to restore the imprest		

(a) Complete and balance the petty cash book for the month of September, using the following analysis columns: **Postage, Stationery, Cleaning, Travel** and **Sundries**, and restore the imprest. Show the posting of the totals of the analysis columns to their accounts in the ledger.

(b) How much will the petty cashier receive to allow him to start October with an imprest of €300?

13 The petty cashier Lauren Costelloe uses a petty cash book to keep an account of small office expenses. She begins each month with an imprest of €200. Here is what happened in May 2012.

May 2012	Details	Voucher no.	€
1	Balance		200.00
4	Bought stationery	1	14.50
5	Bought postage stamps	2	22.00
9	Paid for employee's fare (business)	3	16.00
10	Paid for office cleaning materials	4	12.60
14	Bought postage stamps	5	16.50
18	Bought office stationery	6	24.20
19	Paid for tea/coffee for the office	7	16.70
22	Paid for cleaning materials	8	8.80
24	Paid for employee's fare (business)	9	16.00
26	Bought postage stamps	10	22.00
29	Paid for cleaner	11	28.00
31	Received a cheque to restore the imprest		

(a) Complete and balance the petty cash book for the month of May, using the following analysis columns: **Postage, Stationery, Cleaning, Travel** and **Sundries**, and restore the imprest. Show the posting of the totals of the analysis columns to their accounts in the ledger.

(b) Complete the petty cash voucher for 9 May 2012 submitted by Peter Hayes.

PETTY CASH VOUCHER

No.:
Date:

Details	Amount €

Signature:

Petty Cashier:

14 The petty cashier Kyle Donnelly uses a petty cash book to keep an account of small office expenses. He begins each month with an imprest of €160. Here is what happened in October 2012.

Oct 2012	Details	Voucher no.	€
1	Balance		160.00
3	Bought postage stamps	1	11.00
6	Paid for stationery	2	14.50
9	Paid for office cleaning	3	25.00
12	Bought postage stamps	4	11.00
18	Paid for tea/coffee for the office	5	9.50
19	Paid for cleaning materials	6	7.80
22	Paid for employee's fare (business)	7	12.50
24	Bought postage stamps	8	16.50
26	Paid for stationery	9	13.60
29	Paid a donation to a local charity	10	15.00
31	Received a cheque to restore the imprest		

(a) Complete and balance the petty cash book for the month of October, using the following analysis columns: **Postage**, **Stationery**, **Cleaning**, **Travel** and **Sundries**, and restore the imprest. Show the posting of the totals of the analysis columns to their accounts in the ledger.

(b) Complete the petty cash voucher for 29 October 2012 submitted by Anna Stasiak.

PETTY CASH VOUCHER	No.: Date:
Details	**Amount €**
Signature:	
Petty Cashier:	

15 The petty cashier Karen Peters uses a petty cash book to keep an account of small office expenses. She begins each month with an imprest of €220. Here is what happened in December 2012.

Dec 2012	Details	Voucher no.	€
1	Balance		200.00
3	Bought postage stamps	1	16.50
5	Bought tea/coffee for the office	2	14.20
8	Paid for taxi fare (business)	3	15.00
9	Paid for office cleaning	4	27.00
11	Bought stationery	5	15.80
13	Paid for postage stamps	6	16.50
15	Bought decorations for the office	7	22.60
17	Paid for repairs (office equipment)	8	30.00
22	Paid for post courier service	9	15.00
23	Bought cake for the office	10	12.50
29	Bought postage stamps	11	16.50
31	Received a cheque to restore the imprest		

(a) Complete and balance the petty cash book for the month of December, using the following analysis columns: **Postage, Stationery, Cleaning, Travel** and **Sundries**, and restore the imprest. Show the posting of the totals of the analysis columns to their accounts in the ledger.

(b) Complete the petty cash voucher for 15 December 2012 submitted by Adrian Murphy.

PETTY CASH VOUCHER

No.:
Date:

Details	Amount €

Signature:

Petty Cashier:

16 The petty cashier Peter Zerdal uses a petty cash book to keep an account of small office expenses.
He begins each month with an imprest of €240. Here is what happened in July 2012.

July 2012	Details	Voucher no.	€
1	Balance		240.00
3	Paid for postage stamps	1	27.50
6	Paid for office stationery	2	18.00
8	Paid for registered parcel delivery	3	9.40
11	Bought office groceries	4	15.60
13	Paid for cleaning materials	5	11.80
17	Bought postage stamps	6	16.50
19	Paid the window cleaner	7	24.00
23	Bought ink cartridge refills	8	35.00
25	Paid for taxi fare (business)	9	18.00
29	Bought postage stamps	10	27.50
31	Received a cheque to restore the imprest		

(a) Complete and balance the petty cash book for the month of July, using the following analysis columns: **Postage, Cleaning, Stationery** and **Other Expenses**, and restore the imprest. Show the posting of the totals of the analysis columns to their accounts in the ledger.

(b) Complete petty cash voucher no. 8 (submitted by Kate O'Keeffe).

(c) Briefly explain the purpose of a petty cash voucher.

PETTY CASH VOUCHER

No.:
Date:

Details	Amount €

Signature:

Petty Cashier:

Enquiry, Quotation, Order

Exercises Based on Chapter Content

1 Using the information in Chapter 29 (pages 277–282) of the textbook, answer the following questions.

(a) How many 'Guide to Britain' books did Rainforest Books enquire about? _____

(b) Who is the Managing Director of Rainforest Books? _____

(c) What is the VAT number of Rainforest Books? _____

(d) How much is a 'Guide to Holland' in quotation No. 709? _____

(e) Explain trade discount. _____

_____

_____

(f) Which of the following is the most expensive: ex works, FOB or FOR? _____

(g) What is the price of 'Driving Map of Spain' from Nottinghill Books? _____

(h) What is the cash discount offered by Maps 'N' Books? _____

(i) What is the address of Seasons Books? _____

2 What is the purpose of an order? _____

3 When did Rainforest Books Ltd order goods on order No. 56? _____

4 What is the procedure for dealing with incoming orders received?

_____

_____

_____

5 List four methods used to find a supplier of goods.

(a) _____

(b) _____

(c) _____

(d) _____

Invoice

Exercises Based on Chapter Content

1 What details are shown on an invoice? _____

_____

2 Using the information on page 286 of the textbook, what item was out of stock when Rainforest Books Ltd

ordered goods from Travel Books Ltd? _____

3 Using the information on page 286 of the textbook, what is the number of the invoice sent on 30 March 2011?

_____

4 Is the following statement true or false?
'On an invoice, trade discount is shown first and then VAT is added on'. _____

5 Why are there three copies of a delivery note? _____

_____

6 Why is it a good idea to write 'received but not examined' on a delivery docket? _____

_____

7 Using the information on page 287 of the textbook, what is the number of the delivery note of 6 April 2011

sent by Travel Books Ltd? _____

8 Why should the goods received and the delivery note be compared carefully? _____

_____

9 What is the difference between cash and credit? _____

_____

10 Why is it a good idea to have a good credit rating? _____

_____

11 List three ways that could be used to check a customer's credit rating?

(a) _____

(b) _____

(c) _____

12 Why does a bad debt mean bad news? _____

_____

13 What do businesses offer in order to encourage early payment on a credit invoice? _____

_____

14 Use the following invoice to answer Question 7 on page 290 of the textbook.

Invoice

No. _____

_____

_____

_____

_____

_____

_____

Date: _____

Quantity	Description	Price per unit (€)	Total (€)

Less trade discount _____

Plus VAT _____

Less trade discount %
Plus VAT @ %

Terms: _____
E & OE

15 Use the following invoice to answer Question 8 on page 290 of the textbook.

Invoice

No. _____

_____

_____

_____

_____

_____

_____

_____

Date: _____

Quantity	Description	Price per unit (€)	Total (€)

Less trade discount _____

Plus VAT _____

Less trade discount %
Plus VAT @ %

Terms: _____
E & OE

16 Use the following invoice to answer Question 9 on page 290 of the textbook.

Invoice

No. _____

_____

_____

_____

_____

_____

_____

_____

Date: _____

Quantity	Description	Price per unit (€)	Total (€)

Less trade discount _____

Plus VAT _____

Less trade discount %
Plus VAT @ %

Terms: _____
E & OE

Credit Notes/Debit Notes and Statement of Account

CHAPTER 31

Exercises Based on Chapter Content

1 Name two documents used to correct errors made in business transactions.

(a) _____

(b) _____

2 Match the following with the correct definition.

1	Debit note	A	Decreases the amount due.
2	Credit note	B	Sums up the transactions between firms.
3	Statement of account	C	Corrects an undercharge.

1	2	3

3 Complete the following sentence.

If a cash customer is overcharged for any reason, they are given a _____ refund.

4 What error did Travel Books Ltd discover on invoice no. 4711 (see page 291 of the textbook)?

_____

5 Why did Travel Books Ltd issue a debit note to Rainforest Books Ltd on 11 April 2011?

_____

6 Complete the following sentences by filling in the missing words (see page 293 of the textbook).

How a firm deals with incoming statements

(a) Check that all _____ are included by comparing the statement with the documents on file,

e.g. the quotation, _____, credit and debit notes.

(b) Check all _____.

(c) Compare the statement with the book-keeping records e.g. the creditors' ledger

(_____ is a person who is owed money).

(d) Pay the statement's final figure promptly and avail of any _____ on offer.

(e) File the _____ carefully.

7 How much did Rainforest Books Ltd owe Travel Books Ltd on the following dates (use the statement of account on page 293 of the textbook).

30 March 2011: _____

5 April 2011: _____

11 April 2011: _____

8 Which column in a statement increases the amount due? _____

9 Draft a statement of account for (a) Moore Street Traders and (b) J. Woulfe Ltd using the information in Question 10 on page 296 of the textbook.

(a)

Statement of Account

No. _____

To

_____

_____

_____

_____

_____

_____

_____

Date	Details	Debit (€)	Credit (€)	Balance (€)
				The last figure shown is the amount due

(b)

Statement of Account

No. _____

To

_____

_____

_____

_____

_____

_____

_____

Date	Details	Debit (€)	Credit (€)	Balance (€)
				The last figure shown is the amount due

Cheque and Receipt

Exercises Based on Chapter Content

1 Why is paying by cheque a good idea? _____

_____

2 Fill in the blanks in the following sentences (see page 297 of the textbook).

When a statement of _____ is received it must be checked. Calculations, dates and

document numbers are examined. If all items are _____ the statement is sent to the

_____ department for payment. Bills, statements, etc. are usually paid by

_____ as it is proof of payment. A cheque is an order to the _____

that holds the firm's _____ account to pay money.

3 Fill in the following cheque using the details on the counterfoil.

Date: 2 May 2011			
To: Travel Books Ltd			
For: Statement No. 1948			
Balance	8,700		
Am't Lodged			
Total	8,700		
This Cheque	612.36		
Bal. Forward	8,087.64		
00009761			

A. counterfoil/stub

AIB Bank   43-76-90
MAIN STREET, OOLA, CO. LIMERICK

Date _____

Pay: _____   OR ORDER

_____   € _____

_____   RAINFOREST BOOKS

_____
JANE GRISHAM / RAINFOREST BOOKS

00009761   97429765   34-76-90

B. cheque

4 Fill in the receipt using details from the cheque in Question 3. Travel Books Ltd are entitled to a discount of €68.04 as they paid quickly.

Receipt

No. 477

To
_____
_____
_____

Travel Books Ltd
Unit 8, Davitt Business Park
Castlebar, Co. Mayo

4 May 2011

Received from _____

By Cash	☐	Balance	€ _____
By Cheque	☑	Discount	€ _____
By Credit Card	☐	Cheque	€ _____

Signed   Lenny Planet
Cashier

5 Complete this cheque, paid to Argos for a camera. The price is €320.

Date: 14 April 2011	
To:	
For:	
Balance	2,300
Am't Lodged	/
Total	2,300
This Cheque	
Bal. Forward	
0034561	

AIB Bank
MAIN STREET, ABBEYFEALE, CO. LIMERICK

43-76-90

Date

Pay:

OR ORDER

€

CARLA CONNORS

0798768   20489765   78-76-80

6 Compete this cheque, paid to Sole Lovely shoe shop for wedding shoes. The cost is €125.

Date: 31 January 2011	
To:	
For:	
Balance	3,000
Am't Lodged	/
Total	3,000
This Cheque	
Bal. Forward	
002019441	

Bank of Ireland
MAIN STREET, KILDYSART, CO. CLARE

34-78-10

Date

Pay:

OR ORDER

€

JOHN B. O'CONNOR

00001849   97424758   12-76-00

7 Complete fully the following cheque by writing in anything that is missing.

Date:	
To: Travel Books	
For: Statement No. 1948	
Balance	8,700
Am't Lodged	/
Total	8,700
This Cheque	
Bal. Forward	
00009761	

AIB Bank
MAIN STREET, OOLA, CO. LIMERICK

89-66-92

Date 2/5/2011

Pay:
Six hundred and twelve euro
and thirty six cent

OR ORDER

€ 612.36

RAINFOREST BOOKS LTD

Jane Grisham

00009761   97429765   34-76-90

8 What procedures would you recommend to a business when processing orders received?

_____

_____

9 Other than the price of goods, trade discount and the rate of VAT, name three pieces of information that the purchaser would expect to find in a quotation.

(a) _____

(b) _____

(c) _____

10 Complete the following invoice.

Total (excluding VAT)	€2,300
Trade discount 20%	
Subtotal	
VAT 12%	
Total (including VAT)	

11 Why do firms sell on credit? _____

_____

_____

12 List three methods of checking a new customer's credit rating.

(a) _____

(b) _____

(c) _____

13 What is the procedure for dealing with outgoing statements? _____

_____

_____

Purchases Day Book and Purchases Returns Day Book

1 Tick the boxes (✔) to indicate **true** or **false**.

	True	False
(a) Trading goods are goods for resale in a business.		
(b) An example of a trading good is the computer in a newsagents.		
(c) Credit notes are issued by the seller for returned or damaged goods.		
(d) Credit notes increase the amount to be paid to the seller.		
(e) A creditor is a person/business we owe money to.		
(f) An invoice is another word for a receipt.		

2 Tick (✔) the appropriate column to indicate whether the following are examples of trading or non-trading goods.

	Trading goods	Non-trading goods
Petrol or diesel in a garage.		
Display cabinet in a grocery store.		
Potatoes for sale from a tillage farmer.		
Tools in a hardware store.		
Mechanic's tools in a garage.		

3 Explain the following terms.

(a) Credit: _____

_____

(b) Trading goods: _____

_____

(c) Purchases day book: _____

_____

(d) Creditors: _____

_____

(e) Invoice: _____

_____

4 Enter the correct word, from the list, in the appropriate space in the following sentences.

When buying on credit, the buyer will receive an _____ from the seller, giving the quantity,

description and _____ of the goods. The buyer will then record this credit transaction in

the _____, and will post the details to the _____ ledger.

| cash book | invoice | creditors |
| price | purchases book | credit note |

5 Complete the purchases day book, post the relevant figures to their ledger accounts and extract a trial balance.

Purchases Day Book

Date	Details	Invoice	F	Net	VAT.	Total
2012				€	€	€
8 May	Murdock Ltd	215	CL1	800	172	972
23 May	Emil Supplies Ltd	97	CL2	2,000	430	2,430
				GL1	GL2	

6 Complete the purchases day book, post the relevant figures to their ledger accounts and extract a trial balance.

Purchases Day Book

Date	Details	Invoice	F	Net	VAT	Total
2012				€	€	€
16 June	Reaper & Co Ltd	41	CL1	3,000	405	3,405
24 June	Egnaro Ltd	23	CL2	8,400	1,134	9,534
				GL1	GL2	

7 Complete the purchases day book, including VAT @ 21%, post the relevant figures to their ledger accounts and extract a trial balance.

Purchases Day Book

Date	Details	Invoice	F	Net	VAT	Total
2012				€	€	€
2 July	Mesa Supplies Ltd	98	CL1	4,200		
10 July	Furniture Products Ltd	64	CL2	7,000		
26 July	Mesa Supplies Ltd	111	CL1	6,200		
				GL1	GL2	

8 Enter the following transactions in the purchases day book, post to the ledgers, and extract a trial balance at the end of the month of the current year (excluding VAT @ 21%).

4 March	Purchased goods on credit from Resource Ltd, invoice no. 98	€12,000
12 March	Purchased goods on credit from Karam Ltd, invoice no. 74	€9,000
21 March	Purchased goods on credit from Resource Ltd, invoice no. 121	€10,000

Purchases Day Book

Date	Details	Invoice	F	Net	VAT	Total
				€	€	€
				GL1	GL2	

9 Enter the following transactions in the purchases day book, post to the ledgers, and extract a trial balance at the end of the month of the current year (excluding VAT @ 21%).

8 Jan	Purchased goods on credit from Apex Ltd, invoice no. 64	€6,400
12 Jan	Bought goods on credit from Ole Ltd, invoice no. 79	€8,000
16 Jan	Purchased goods on credit from Apex Ltd, invoice no. 98	€7,600
24 Jan	Bought goods on credit from Ole Ltd, invoice no. 98	€5,200

Purchases Day Book

Date	Details	Invoice	F	Net	VAT	Total
				€	€	€
				GL1	GL2	

10 Enter the following transactions in the purchases day book, post to the ledgers, and extract a trial balance at the end of the month of the current year (excluding VAT @ 21%).

5 Feb	Purchased goods on credit from Parkinson & Co, invoice no. 64	€7,200
11 Feb	Purchased goods on credit from Robinson Ltd, invoice no. 75	€10,000
18 Feb	Purchased goods on credit from Parkinson & Co, invoice no. 78	€5,500
26 Feb	Purchased goods on credit from Berger Ltd, invoice no. 134	€2,400

11 Enter the following transactions in the purchases day book, post to the ledgers, and extract a trial balance at the end of the month of the current year (excluding VAT @ 21%).

5 April	Purchased goods on credit from Fern Ltd, invoice no. 76	€7,200
11 April	Purchased goods on credit from Thistle Ltd, invoice no. 45	€14,000
17 April	Purchased goods on credit from Rose Ltd, invoice no. 59	€5,000
26 April	Purchased goods on credit from Fern Ltd, invoice no. 104	€6,000

12 Enter the following transactions in the purchases day book, post to the ledgers, and extract a trial balance at the end of the month of the current year (excluding VAT @ 21%).

4 Aug	Bought goods on credit from Royal Ltd, invoice no. 165	€9,500
9 Aug	Purchased goods on credit from Minion Ltd, invoice no. 146	€15,000
16 Aug	Purchased goods on credit from Royal Ltd, invoice no. 206	€6,000
22 Aug	Purchased goods on credit from Joker Supplies, invoice no. 139	€16,000
28 Aug	Received invoice no. 201, for goods bought on credit from King Ltd	€7,200

13 Enter the following transactions in the purchases day book, post to the ledgers, and extract a trial balance at the end of the month of the current year (excluding VAT @ 21%).

5 Oct	Purchased goods on credit from Gosil Supplies Ltd, invoice no. 403	€4,000
11 Oct	Purchased goods on credit from Oyam Ltd, invoice no. 202	€5,600
17 Oct	Purchased goods on credit from Rock Ltd, invoice no. 157	€6,400
25 Oct	Purchased goods on credit from Gosil Supplies Ltd, invoice no. 457	€5,200

14 Explain the following terms.

(a) Credit note: _____

_____

(b) Purchases returns book: _____

_____

15 Complete the purchases returns books, post to the ledger accounts and extract a trial balance.

Purchases Returns Day Book

Date	Details	Credit Note	F	Net	VAT	Total
2012				€	€	€
6 May	Techniks Ltd	31	CL1	260	35.10	
15 May	Automaton Ltd	14	CL2	140	18.90	
				GL1	GL2	

16 Complete the purchases returns books below, post to the ledger accounts and extract a trial balance.

Purchases Returns Day Book

Date	Details	Credit Note	F	Net	VAT	Total
2012				€	€	€
7 Nov	Yeats Ltd	63	CL1	400	86.00	
18 Nov	Shaw Ltd	17	CL2	160	34.40	
				GL1	GL2	

17 Complete the following transactions in the purchases book and the purchases returns book, post to the ledgers, and extract a trial balance at the end of the month of the current year (excluding VAT @ 21%).

Purchases Day Book

Date	Details	Invoice	F	Net	VAT	Total
				€	€	€
4 May	Rice Ltd	187	CL1	4,000		
10 May	Broderick Ltd	210	CL2	3,400		
18 May	Rice Ltd	218	CL1	4,800		
				GL1	GL2	

Purchases Returns Day Book

Date	Details	Credit Note	F	Net	VAT	Total
				€	€	€
22 May	Rice Ltd	43	CL1	200		
				GL3	GL2	

18 Complete the following transactions in the purchases book and the purchases returns book, post to the ledgers, and extract a trial balance at the end of the month of the current year (excluding VAT @ 21%).

Purchases Day Book

Date	Details	Invoice	F	Net	VAT	Total
				€	€	€
3 March	Ryan & Co. Ltd	92	CL1	9,200		
12 March	Tardel Ltd	50	CL2	10,600		
24 March	Ryan & Co. Ltd	108	CL1	7,800		
				GL1	GL2	

Purchases Returns Day Book

Date	Details	Credit Note	F	Net	VAT	Total
				€	€	€
15 March	Tardel Ltd	15	CL2	800		
28 March	Ryan & Co. Ltd	23	CL1	500		
				GL3	GL2	

19 Enter the following transactions in the purchases book and purchases returns book, post to the ledgers, and extract a trial balance at the end of the month (current year) (excl. VAT @ 13.5%).

5 Feb	Purchased goods on credit from Carrot Ltd, invoice no. 37	€14,000
9 Feb	Purchased goods on credit from Trent plc, invoice no. 29	€18,000
13 Feb	Returned goods to Trent plc, credit note no. 9	€2,400
24 Feb	Purchased goods on credit from Carrot Ltd, invoice no. 49	€11,000

20 Enter the following transactions in the purchases book and purchases returns book, post to the ledgers, and extract a trial balance at the end of the month (current year) (excl. VAT @ 13.5%).

3 Dec	Purchased goods on credit from Office Supplies Ltd, invoice no. 289	€8,000
9 Dec	Purchased goods on credit from Fern Ltd, invoice no. 322	€6,200
12 Dec	Returned goods to Office Supplies Ltd, credit note no. 51	€350
19 Dec	Purchased goods on credit from Office Supplies Ltd, invoice no. 318	€7,200
22 Dec	Bought goods on credit from Fern Ltd, invoice no. 384	€2,800

21 Enter the following transactions in the purchases book and purchases returns book, post to the ledgers, and extract a trial balance at the end of the month (current year) (excl. VAT @ 13.5%).

4 Jan	Purchased goods on credit from Logic Ltd, invoice no. 1	€15,000
6 Jan	Returned goods to Logic Ltd, credit note no. 1	€500
9 Jan	Purchased goods on credit from Solutions Ltd, invoice no. 9	€3,300
11 Jan	Returned goods to Solutions Ltd, credit note no. 3	€100
16 Jan	Purchased goods on credit from Logic Ltd, invoice no. 18	€8,000
24 Jan	Bought goods on credit from Solutions Ltd, invoice no. 16	€2,700

22 Complete the following transactions in the books of first entry, post to the ledgers, balance the accounts and extract a trial balance at the end of the month (current year) (excl. VAT @ 21%).

Purchases Day Book

Date	Details	Invoice	F	Net	VAT	Total
				€	€	€
5 April	Roche & Co. Ltd	186	CL1	7,200		
9 April	Endline Resources	71	CL2	6,000		
15 April	Roche & Co. Ltd	204	CL1	5,800		
23 April	Endline Resources	84	CL2	4,000		
				GL1	GL2	

Purchases Returns Day Book

Date	Details	Credit Note	F	Net	VAT	Total
				€	€	€
7 April	Roche & Co. Ltd	12	CL1	200		
12 April	Endline Resources	21	CL2	260		
				GL3	GL2	

Dr   **Cash Book**   **Cr**

Date	Details	F	Bank	Date	Details	Chq	F	Bank	Creditor
			€					€	€
				20 April	Roche & Co. Ltd	28	CL1	10,000	
				28 April	Endline Resources	29	CL2	7,500	

23 Enter the following transactions in the appropriate books of first entry, post to the ledgers, balance the accounts and extract a trial balance at the end of the month (current year) (excl. VAT @ 21%).

4 Feb	Purchased goods on credit from Axle Ltd, invoice no. 12	€4,200
7 Feb	Purchased goods on credit from Car Parts Ltd, invoice no. 44	€5,600
10 Feb	Returned goods to Car Parts Ltd (damaged), credit note no. 8	€600
20 Feb	Purchased goods on credit from Axle Ltd, invoice no. 21	€3,400
22 Feb	Returned goods to Axle Ltd (not as ordered), credit note no. 5	€200
24 Feb	Purchased goods on credit from Car Parts Ltd, invoice no. 62	€3,800
26 Feb	Paid Axle Ltd, by cheque no. 23	€5,200
28 Feb	Paid Car Parts Ltd, by cheque no. 24	€6,000

24 Enter the following transactions in the appropriate books of first entry, post to the ledgers, balance the accounts and extract a trial balance at the end of the month (current year) (excl. VAT @ 21%).

2 March	Purchased goods on credit from Winters & Co Ltd, invoice no. 42	€9,000
6 March	Purchased goods on credit from Spring Ltd, invoice no. 38	€6,000
9 March	Returned goods to Spring Ltd (not ordered), credit note no. 11	€1,000
15 March	Purchased goods on credit from All Seasons Ltd, invoice no. 63	€4,000
24 March	Paid Winters & Co Ltd, by cheque no. 24	€7,000
26 March	Paid Spring Ltd, by cheque no. 25	€4,000

25 Enter the following transactions in the appropriate books of first entry, post to the ledgers, balance the accounts and extract a trial balance at the end of the month (current year) (excl. VAT @ 21%).

2 June	Purchased goods on credit from Baker Ltd, invoice no. 128	€25,000
5 June	Purchased goods on credit from Onion Ltd, invoice no. 83	€16,000
9 June	Paid Baker Ltd on account, by cheque no. 36	€15,000
16 June	Bought goods on credit from Carlton Ltd, invoice no. 114	€18,000
19 June	Received a credit note no. 17 from Carlton Ltd for returned goods	€2,000
21 June	Paid Onion Ltd, by cheque no. 37, in full settlement of the amount due	
28 June	Paid Carlton Ltd on account, by cheque no. 38	€10,000

26 Enter the following transactions in the appropriate books of first entry, post to the ledgers, balance the accounts and extract a trial balance at the end of the month (current year) (excl. VAT @ 21%).

3 April	Purchased goods on credit from Delaware Ltd, invoice no. 41	€9,000
7 April	Purchased goods on credit from Nevada Ltd, invoice no. 18	€4,500
9 April	Paid Delaware Ltd by cheque no. 19, in full settlement	
11 April	Received a credit note no.18, from Nevada Ltd for returned goods	€600
14 April	Bought goods on credit from Delaware Ltd, invoice no. 57	€7,500
20 April	Paid Nevada Ltd, by cheque no. 20, in full settlement of the amount due	
23 April	Purchased goods on credit from Delaware Ltd, invoice no. 75	€6,750
29 April	Paid Delaware Ltd on account, by cheque no. 21	€9,750

27 Enter the following transactions in the appropriate books of first entry, post to the ledgers, balance the accounts and extract a trial balance at the end of the month (current year) (excl. VAT @ 21%).

5 Feb	Purchased goods on credit from Equipment Supplies Ltd, invoice no. 54	€16,000
7 Feb	Returned goods to Equipment Supplies Ltd (damaged), credit note no. 17,	€1,000
10 Feb	Purchased goods on credit from Metal Manufacturers Ltd, invoice no. 92	€20,000
15 Feb	Paid Equipment Supplies Ltd on account, by cheque no. 17	€11,000
20 Feb	Purchased goods on credit from Metal Manufacturers Ltd, invoice no. 102	€14,000
24 Feb	Returned goods to Metal Manufacturers Ltd, credit note no. 16	€1,600
28 Feb	Paid Metal Manufacturers Ltd, by cheque no. 18, in full settlement	

28 What is the purpose of the Creditors Control Account?

_____

_____

_____

29 Complete and balance the creditors' control account from the following data.

30 April	Total purchases on credit	€112,600
30 April	Total as per the purchases returns book	€4,300
30 April	Total paid, by cheque, to creditors	€95,000

Creditors' Control Account

Date	Details	F	Dr	Cr	Balance
2012			€	€	€
1 April	Balance				27,000

30 Complete and balance the creditors' control account from the following data.

31 May	Total purchases on credit	€54,000
31 May	Total as per the purchases returns book	€700
31 May	Total paid, by cheque, to creditors	€60,000

Creditors' Control Account

Date	Details	F	Dr	Cr	Balance
2012			€	€	€
1 May	Balance				13,000

31 Complete and balance the creditors' control account from the following data.

30 June	Total purchases on credit	€33,100
30 June	Total cash purchases	€11,600
30 June	Total as per the purchases returns book	€2,100
30 June	Total paid, by cheque, to creditors	€35,000

Creditors' Control Account

Date	Details	F	Dr	Cr	Balance
			€	€	€
1 June	Balance				8,400

32 Complete and balance the creditors' control account from the following data.

Total purchases on credit in July	€60,480
Total payments (by cheque) during July to creditors	€55,200
Cash purchases during July	€6,048

Creditors' Control Account

Dr ... **Cr**

Date	Details	€	Date	Details	€
			1 July	Balance	11,520

33 Complete and balance the creditors' control account from the following data.

31 Aug	Total purchases on credit	€61,920
31 Aug	Total cash purchases	€24,960
31 Aug	Total as per the purchases returns book	€4,320
31 Aug	Total paid, by cheque, to creditors	€50,400

Creditors' Control Account

Date	Details	F	Debit	Credit	Balance
2012			€	€	€
1 Aug	Balance				80,640

34 The following account appears in the creditors' ledger of J. Browning Ltd.

Date 2012	Details	F	Total €	Date 2012	Details	F	Total €
				Smith & Co. Ltd A/C			
13/5	Returns	PRB	600	1/5	Balance	b/d	2,400
20/5	Bank	CB	5,000	9/5	Purchases	PB	3,600

(a) Balance the above account.
(b) Complete the following sentences to explain the entries in the account.

On 1 May J. Browning _____

_____

On 9 May J. Browning _____

_____

On 20 May J. Browning _____

_____

35 The following account appears in the creditors' ledger of T. Dixon Ltd.

Date 2013	Details	F	Total €	Date 2013	Details	F	Total €
				Hardware Ltd A/C			
10/6	Returns	PRB	400	1/6	Balance	b/d	7,100
17/6	Bank	CB	10,000	8/6	Purchases	PB	8,400

(a) Balance the above account.
(b) Complete the following sentences to explain the entries in the account.

On 1 June T. Dixon _____

_____

On 10 June T. Dixon _____

_____

On 17 June T. Dixon _____

_____

36   Convert 'Smith & Co A/C' (Question 34) and 'Hardware Ltd A/C' (Question 35) into continuous layout.

Smith & Co A/C

Date	Details	F	Debit	Credit	Balance
2012			€	€	€
1/5	Balance	b/d			2,400

Hardware Ltd A/C

Date	Details	F	Debit	Credit	Balance
2013			€	€	€
1/6	Balance	b/d			7,100

CHAPTER 34

Sales Day Book and Sales Returns Day Book

1 Tick the boxes (✔) to indicate **true** or **false**.

	True	False
(a) An order document is sent by the seller giving instructions to the buyer.		
(b) A debtor owes us money, and is an asset to the business.		
(c) The sales day book records all sales, cash and credit.		
(d) An example of a non-trading good is buying a forklift for use in the warehouse.		
(e) 'Cash discount 10% in 7 days' will give 10% off if paid in the next 7 days.		

2 Outline the steps that a business should go through on receiving an order for credit sales.

(a) _____

(b) _____

(c) _____

(d) _____

(e) _____

(f) _____

(g) _____

3 Explain the following terms.

(a) Debtor: _____

_____

(b) Trading goods: _____

_____

(c) Sales day book: _____

_____

(d) Sales returns book: _____

_____

4 Identify one advantage and one disadvantage of selling goods on credit.

Advantage: _____

_____

Disadvantage: _____

_____

5 Complete the sales book, post the relevant figures to their ledger accounts and extract a trial balance.

Sales Day Book

Date	Details	Invoice	F	Net	VAT	Total
2012				€	€	€
6 April	Mallon Ltd	97	DL1	4,200	567	
20 April	Tigris Ltd	98	DL2	7,400	999	
				GL1	GL2	

6 Complete the sales book, post the relevant figures to their ledger accounts and extract a trial balance.

Sales Day Book

Date	Details	Invoice	F	Net	VAT	Total
2012				€	€	€
6 May	Dreamcast Ltd	167	DL1	5,600	756	
17 May	Weaver & Co. Ltd	168	DL2	2,200	297	
				GL1	GL2	

7 Complete the sales day book, including VAT @ 21%, post the relevant figures to their ledger accounts and extract a trial balance.

Sales Day Book

Date	Details	Invoice	F	Net	VAT	Total
2012				€	€	€
6 Aug	Lolly Ltd	98	DL1	4,200		
12 Aug	Sweet & Co.	99	DL2	7,000		
21 Aug	Lolly Ltd	100	DL1	6,200		
				GL1	GL2	

8 Enter the following transactions in the sales day book, post to the ledgers, and extract a trial balance at the end of the month of the current year (excluding VAT @ 21%).

3 Sept	Sold goods on credit to Rawling Ltd, invoice no. 238	€14,000
14 Sept	Sold goods on credit to Knock Ltd, invoice no. 239	€8,000
22 Sept	Sold goods on credit to Rawling Ltd, invoice no. 240	€11,000

Sales Day Book

Date	Details	Invoice	F	Net €	VAT €	Total €
				GL1	GL2	

9 Enter the following transactions in the sales day book, post to the ledgers, and extract a trial balance at the end of the month of the current year (excluding VAT @ 21%).

8 Oct	Sold goods on credit to Truck Sales Ltd, invoice no. 329	€7,200
16 Oct	Sold goods on credit to Car Parts Ltd, invoice no. 330	€2,600
23 Oct	Sold goods on credit to Truck Sales Ltd, invoice no. 331	€6,000
28 Oct	Sold goods on credit to Valeting Services Ltd, invoice no. 332	€1,800

Sales Day Book

Date	Details	Invoice	F	Net €	VAT €	Total €
				GL1	GL2	

10 Enter the following transactions in the sales day book, post to the ledgers, and extract a trial balance at the end of the month of the current year (excluding VAT @ 21%).

4 Nov	Sold goods on credit to Pineview Ltd, invoice no. 383	€4,800
12 Nov	Sold goods on credit to Palance & Co. Ltd, invoice no. 384	€4,000
20 Nov	Sold goods on credit to Pineview Ltd, invoice no. 385	€3,200
24 Nov	Sold goods on credit to Palance & Co. Ltd, invoice no. 386	€2,100

Sales Day Book

Date	Details	Invoice	F	Net €	VAT €	Total €
				GL1	GL2	

11   Enter the following transactions in the sales day book, post to the ledgers, and extract a trial balance at the end of the month of the current year (excluding VAT @ 13.5%).

4 Dec	Sold goods on credit to Amigo & Co., invoice no. 414	€8,400
16 Dec	Sold goods on credit to Cara Ltd, invoice no. 415	€6,700
19 Dec	Sold goods on credit to Amigo & Co., invoice no. 416	€7,100

12   Enter the following transactions in the sales day book, post to the ledgers, and extract a trial balance at the end of the month of the current year (excluding VAT @ 13.5%).

5 Jan	Sold goods on credit to Fitzgerald Ltd, invoice no. 1	€1,400
9 Jan	Sold goods on credit to Primula Ltd, invoice no. 2	€1,900
15 Jan	Sold goods on credit to Fitzgerald Ltd, invoice no. 3	€2,100
23 Jan	Sold goods on credit to Blossoms Ltd, invoice no. 4	€800

13   Complete the sales returns books below, post to the ledger accounts and extract a trial balance.

Sales Returns Day Book

Date	Details	Credit note	F	Net	VAT	Total
2012				€	€	€
3 Feb	Techs Ltd	13	DL1	300	64.50	
14 Feb	Auto Ltd	14	DL2	400	86.00	
				GL1	GL2	

14   Complete the sales returns books below, post to the ledger accounts and extract a trial balance.

Sales Returns Day Book

Date	Details	Credit note	F	Net	VAT	Total
2013				€	€	€
9 March	King & Co. Ltd	28	DL1	220	29.70	
24 March	Prince Ltd	29	DL2	80	10.80	
				GL1	GL2	

15   Complete the following transactions in the sales book and the sales returns book, post to the ledgers, and extract a trial balance at the end of the month of the current year (excluding VAT @ 21%).

Sales Day Book

Date	Details	Invoice	F	Net	VAT	Total
				€	€	€
3 April	Della Ltd	207	DL1	6,000		
10 April	Bridgeway Ltd	208	DL2	4,400		
20 April	Della Ltd	209	DL1	5,800		
				GL1	GL2	

Sales Returns Day Book

Date	Details	Credit note	F	Net	VAT	Total
				€	€	€
22 April	Della Ltd	14	DL1	500		
				GL3	GL2	

16 Complete the following transactions in the sales book and the sales returns book, post to the ledgers, and extract a trial balance at the end of the month of the current year (excluding VAT @ 21%).

Sales Day Book

Date	Details	Invoice	F	Net	VAT	Total
				€	€	€
6 May	O'Malley & Co. Ltd	106	DL1	1,700		
14 May	Trent Ltd	107	DL2	2,600		
23 May	O'Malley & Co. Ltd	108	DL1	1,400		
				GL1	GL2	

Sales Returns Day Book

Date	Details	Credit note	F	Net	VAT	Total
				€	€	€
16 May	Trent Ltd	18	DL2	200		
26 May	O'Malley & Co. Ltd	19	DL1	220		
				GL3	GL2	

17 Enter the following transactions in the sales book and sales returns book, post to the ledgers, and extract a trial balance at the end of the month (current year) (excl. VAT @ 13.5%).

3 June	Sold goods on credit to Apex Ltd, invoice no. 87	€6,000
8 June	Sold goods on credit to Nadir Ltd, invoice no. 88	€5,200
10 June	Nadir Ltd returned goods (not as ordered), credit note no. 8	€800
19 June	Sold goods on credit to Apex Ltd, invoice no. 89	€4,600
24 June	Sold goods on credit to Vertex & Co., invoice no. 90	€2,600

18 Enter the following transactions in the sales book and sales returns book, post to the ledgers, and extract a trial balance at the end of the month (current year) (excl. VAT @ 13.5%).

2 July	Sold goods on credit to Oakdale Ltd, invoice no. 121	€11,000
9 July	Sold goods on credit to Pineview Ltd, invoice no. 122	€8,100
11 July	Pineview Ltd returned goods, credit note no. 17	€400
16 July	Sold goods on credit to Oakdale Ltd, invoice no. 123	€7,800
19 July	Oakdale Ltd returned goods, credit note no. 18	€600
24 July	Sold goods on credit to Cherrywood Ltd, invoice no. 124	€6,250

19 Enter the following transactions in the sales book and sales returns book, post to the ledgers, and extract a trial balance at the end of the month (current year) (excl. VAT @ 13.5%).

2 Aug	Sold goods on credit to Logen Ltd, invoice no. 341	€24,000
5 Aug	Logen Ltd returned goods (damaged), credit note no. 26	€1,500
12 Aug	Sold goods on credit to Equipment Supplies Ltd, invoice no. 342	€4,800
14 Aug	Equipment Supplies Ltd returned goods, credit note no. 27	€600
24 Aug	Sold goods on credit to Equipment Supplies Ltd, invoice no. 343	€2,400

20 Tick the boxes (✔) to indicate **true** or **false**.

		True	False
(a)	The credit note is used to write up the sales returns book.		
(b)	The sales returns book is for all sales returns, cash and credit.		
(c)	A credit rating can be checked by asking for a bank reference.		
(d)	A credit rating can be checked by asking for a trade reference from other businesses.		
(e)	Goods can be returned if you get a better deal elsewhere.		

21 Complete the following transactions in the books of first entry, post to the ledgers, balance the accounts and extract a trial balance at the end of the month (current year) (excl. VAT @ 21%)

Sales Day Book

Date	Details	Invoice	F	Net	VAT	Total
				€	€	€
4 Sept	Rowling & Co. Ltd	245	DL1	8,000		
8 Sept	Potter Resources Ltd	246	DL2	4,600		
14 Sept	Rowling & Co. Ltd	247	DL1	6,000		
22 Sept	Weasley Ltd	248	DL3	7,000		
				GL1	GL2	

Sales Returns Day Book

Date	Details	Credit note	F	Net	VAT	Total
				€	€	€
6 Sept	Rowling & Co. Ltd	33	DL1	400		
24 Sept	Weasley Ltd	34	DL3	500		
				GL3	GL2	

Cash Book (extract)

Dr   **Cr**

Date	Details	F	Bank	Debtor	Date	Details	Chq	F	Bank
			€	€					€
21 Sept	Rowling & Co.	DL1	10,000	10,000					
29 Sept	Weasley Ltd	DL3	4,500	4,500					

22 Enter the following transactions in the books of first entry, post to the ledgers, balance the accounts and extract a trial balance at the end of the month (current year) (excl. VAT @ 21%).

4 Oct	Sold goods on credit to White & Co. Ltd, invoice no. 271	€9,000
7 Oct	Sold goods on credit to Barry Ltd, invoice no. 272	€6,300
10 Oct	Barry Ltd returned goods (damaged), credit note no. 35	€1,300
18 Oct	Sold goods on credit to Barry Ltd, invoice no. 273	€3,900
22 Oct	White & Co. Ltd paid by cheque on account	€6,600
28 Oct	Barry Ltd paid by cheque in part settlement	€6,500

23 Enter the following transactions in the books of first entry, post to the ledgers, balance the accounts and extract a trial balance at the end of the month (current year) (excl. VAT @ 21%).

3 Nov	Sold goods on credit to Amigo Ltd, invoice no. 371	€12,000
6 Nov	Sold goods on credit to Cairde Ltd, invoice no. 372	€10,000
7 Nov	Amigo Ltd returned goods (not ordered), credit note no. 47	€700
12 Nov	Amigo Ltd paid by cheque in part settlement	€8,500
16 Nov	Sold goods on credit to Friend Ltd, invoice no. 373	€14,000
18 Nov	Friend Ltd returned goods (damaged), credit note no. 48	€600
22 Nov	Cairde Ltd paid on account, by cheque	€7,200
26 Nov	Friend Ltd paid by cheque in full settlement of the amount owed	

24 Enter the following transactions in the books of first entry, post to the ledgers, balance the accounts and extract a trial balance at the end of the month (current year) (excl. VAT @ 21%).

3 Dec	Sold goods on credit to Malin Ltd, invoice no. 524	€15,000
6 Dec	Sold goods on credit to Slea Ltd, invoice no. 525	€10,500
8 Dec	Slea Ltd returned goods, credit note no. 56	€900
13 Dec	Malin Ltd paid on account by cheque	€12,500
15 Dec	Sold goods on credit to Rosses Ltd, invoice no. 526	€9,000
17 Dec	Rosses Ltd returned goods, credit note no. 57	€500
20 Dec	Slea Ltd paid by cheque in full settlement of the amount due	
22 Dec	Rosses Ltd paid on account, by cheque	€6,000

25 Enter the following transactions in the books of first entry, post to the ledgers, balance the accounts and extract a trial balance at the end of the month (current year) (excl. VAT @ 21%).

4 Jan	Sold goods on credit to Data Ltd, invoice no. 1	€8,200
8 Jan	Sold goods on credit to Pointer Ltd, invoice no. 2	€4,500
10 Jan	Pointer Ltd returned goods, credit note no. 1	€200
14 Jan	Pointer Ltd paid by cheque in full settlement	
15 Jan	Sold goods on credit to Data Ltd, invoice no. 3	€6,600
17 Jan	Data Ltd returned goods, credit note no. 2	€420
23 Jan	Sold goods on credit to Data Ltd, invoice no. 4	€4,000
28 Jan	Data Ltd paid by cheque in full settlement	

26 Complete and balance the debtors control account using the following data.

28 Feb	Total sales on credit	€56,800
28 Feb	Total as per the sales returns book	€1,600
28 Feb	Total received, by cheque, from debtors	€48,200

Debtors' Control Account

Date	Details	F	Dr	Cr	Balance
			€	€	€
1 Feb	Balance				9,650

27 Complete and balance the debtors' control account using the following data.

31 March	Total sales on credit	€100,800
31 March	Total as per the sales returns book	€10,560
31 March	Total received, by cheque, from debtors	€99,600

Debtors' Control Account

Date	Details	F	Dr	Cr	Balance
			€	€	€
1 March	Balance				21,600

28 Complete and balance the debtors' control account using the following data.

31 May	Total sales on credit	€60,480
31 May	Total as per the sales returns book	€6,000
31 May	Total received, by cheque, from debtors	€55,200

Dr   Debtors' Control Account   Cr

Date	Details	€	Date	Details	€
1 May	Balance	12,720			

29 Complete and balance the debtors' control account using the following data.

30 June	Total sales on credit	€38,450
30 June	Total cash sales	€72,460
30 June	Total as per the sales returns book	€2,800
30 June	Total received, by cheque, from debtors	€39,200

Debtors' Control Account

Date	Details	F	Dr	Cr	Balance
			€	€	€
1 June	Balance				8,850

30 The following account appeared in the debtors' ledger of Hillview Ltd.

Date 2013	Details	F	Total €	Date 2013	Details	F	Total €
			Baltic Ltd A/C				
1/3	Balance	b/d	800	18/3	Bank	CB	4,700
10/3	Sales	SB	6,100	**31/3**	**Balance**		
			6,900				6,900
1/4	**Balance**						

(a) Balance the above account.

(b) Complete the sentences below to explain the entries in the account:

   (i) On 1 March 2013 Hillview Ltd _____

      _____

   (ii) On 10 March 2013 Hillview Ltd _____

      _____

   (iii) On 18 March 2013 Hillview Ltd _____

      _____

31 The following account appeared in the debtors' ledger of Refix Ltd.

Date 2013	Details	F	Total €	Date 2013	Details	F	Total €
			All Repairs Ltd A/C				
1/4	Balance	b/d	1,700	12/4	Sales Ret	SRB	400
9/4	Sales	SB	8,200	24/4	Bank	CB	7,000
				30/4	**Balance**		
			9,900				9,900
1/5	**Balance**						

(a) Balance the above account.

(b) Complete the sentences below to explain the entries in the account:

  (i) On 1 April 2013 Refix Ltd _____

  _____

  (ii) On 9 April 2013 Refix Ltd _____

  _____

  (iii) On 12 April 2013 Refix Ltd _____

  _____

32 Convert 'Baltic Ltd A/C' (Question 30) and 'All Repairs Ltd A/C' (Question 31) into continuous layout.

Baltic Ltd A/C

Date	Details	F	Dr	Cr	Balance
2013			€	€	€
1/3	Balance	b/d			800

All Repairs Ltd A/C

Date	Details	F	Dr	Cr	Balance
2013			€	€	€
1/4	Balance	b/d			1,700

The General Journal

1 Explain the following terms.

(a) Books of first entry: _____

_____

(b) Assets: _____

_____

(c) Liabilities: _____

_____

(d) Share capital: _____

_____

2 Calculate the share capital, and post the following opening entries to the appropriate ledger accounts.

General Journal

Date	Details	F	Dr €	Cr €
1/1/2013	**Assets:**			
	Premises	GL1	340,000	
	Machinery	GL2	105,000	
	Stock	GL3	17,000	
	Bank	CB	11,500	
	Liabilities:			
	Loan	GL4		23,500
	Ordinary share capital	GL5		
	Assets, liabilities & share capital on this date		473,500	473,500

3 Calculate the share capital, and post the following opening entries to the appropriate ledger accounts.

General Journal

Date	Details	F	Dr €	Cr €
1/2/2013	**Assets:**			
	Premises	GL1	495,000	
	Vehicles	GL2	64,000	
	Stock	GL3	22,600	
	Bank	CB	11,500	
	Liabilities:			
	Creditor: Toomey & Co.	CL1		3,100
	Ordinary share capital	GL4		
	Assets, liabilities & share capital on this date			

4   Record the opening entries in the general journal, calculate the ordinary share capital, and post to the appropriate ledger accounts.
A business has the following assets and liabilities on 1 January 2013:
    Buildings €650,000; Bank Overdraft €5,500; Stock €16,000; Vehicles €48,000; Cash €1,000.

General Journal

Date	Details	F	Dr €	Cr €
1/1/2013	**Assets:**			
	Liabilities:			

5   Record the opening entries in the general journal, calculate the ordinary share capital, and post to the appropriate ledger accounts.
A business has the following assets and liabilities on 1 February 2013:
    Buildings €650,000; Vehicles €65,000; Equipment €78,000; Stock €55,000; Bank €15,000.
    Debtor: O'Sullivan Ltd €12,000.
    Creditors: Aster Ltd €19,000; Apt Supplies Ltd €6,000.

General Journal

Date	Details	F	Dr €	Cr €
1/2/2013	**Assets:**			
	Liabilities:			

6   Record the opening entries in the general journal, calculate the ordinary share capital, and post to the appropriate ledger accounts.
A business has the following assets and liabilities on 1 March 2013:
    Assets: Premises €650,000; Vehicles €82,000; Plant & Machinery €126,000; Stock €35,000; Bank €21,000.
        Debtor: Mornay Ltd €12,000.
    Liabilities: Creditor: Aspil Ltd €6,000; Loan €120,000.

7   Record the opening entries in the general journal, calculate the ordinary share capital, and post to the appropriate ledger accounts.
A business has the following assets and liabilities on 1 April 2013:
    Assets: Vehicles €36,000; Equipment €24,000; Furniture €12,000; Stock €42,000; Bank €9,000.
        Debtor: Morrell & Co. Ltd €4,000.
    Liabilities: Creditor: Repart Ltd €7,000; Loan €20,000.

8   Record the opening entries in the general journal, calculate the ordinary share capital, and post to the appropriate ledger accounts.
A business has the following assets and liabilities on 1 May 2013:
   Assets: Premises €460,000; Vehicles €38,000; Equipment €47,000; Stock €41,000; Cash €4,000.
   Debtor: Bowen & Co. Ltd €7,500.
   Liabilities: Creditor: Jacobs Ltd €6,000; Bank Overdraft €9,500; Loan €82,000.

9   Record the opening entries in the general journal, calculate the ordinary share capital, and post to the appropriate ledger accounts.
A business has the following assets and liabilities on 1 June 2013:
   Assets: Machinery €65,000; Vehicles €28,000; Equipment €14,000; Stock €27,000; Cash €5,500.
   Debtors: Hillcrest & Co. Ltd €6,000; Refit Ltd €3,500.
   Liabilities: Creditor: Malone Ltd €9,000; Bank Overdraft €10,000; Loan €30,000.

Record each of the following 'uncommon entries' in the general journal and post to the relevant ledger accounts (using today's date).

10   O'Brien's Garage Ltd purchased a photocopier on credit from Depot Ltd for €960.

General Journal (of O'Brien's Garage Ltd)

Date	Details	F	Dr €	Cr €
	Equipment A/C To: Depot Ltd A/C i.e. purchase of a photocopier on credit	GL1 CL1		

11   Carolan's Bakery bought a new delivery van on credit from Galway Motors Ltd for €18,000.

General Journal (of Carolan's Bakery)

Date	Details	F	Dr €	Cr €
	Vehicle A/C To: Galway Motors Ltd A/C i.e. purchase of a delivery van on credit	GL1 CL1		

12   Quinn's Garage bought equipment for use in the garage on credit from Ray Engineering for €7,200.

General Journal (of Quinn's Garage)

Date	Details	F	Dr €	Cr €
	 To: i.e.	GL1 CL1		

13 Bayleaf Printers Ltd bought furniture on credit from Office Furniture Ltd for €2,560.

General Journal (of Bayleaf Printers Ltd)

Date	Details	F	Dr €	Cr €
	To: i.e.	GL1 CL1		

14 Dolan Paints bought equipment on credit from Equipment Supplies Ltd for €2,200 (excl. VAT @ 13.5%).

General Journal (of Dolan Paints Ltd)

Date	Details	F	Dr €	Cr €
	To: i.e.	GL1 GL2 CL1		

15 Regal Tiles bought office furniture on credit from Office Resources Ltd for €3,000 (excl. VAT @ 21%).

General Journal (of Regal Tiles)

Date	Details	F	Dr €	Cr €
	To: i.e.	GL1 GL2 CL1		

16 Roper Construction Ltd bought a bulldozer on credit from Kiely's Garage for €30,000 (excl. VAT @ 21%).

General Journal (of Roper Construction Ltd)

Date	Details	F	Dr €	Cr €
	To: i.e.	GL1 GL2 CL1		

Record each of the following 'uncommon entries' in the general journal and post to the relevant ledger accounts (using today's date).

17 A debtor, P. Grogan, who owes €1,450 is declared bankrupt, and the balance is written off as a bad debt.

General Journal

Date	Details	F	Dr €	Cr €
	Bad debts a/c To: P. Grogan i.e. debtor declared bankrupt and debt written off	GL1 DL1		

18 A debtor, Presidio Ltd, who owes €9,100 is declared bankrupt, and the balance is written off as a bad debt.

General Journal

Date	Details	F	Dr €	Cr €
	To: i.e.	GL1 DL1		

19 A debtor, Lake Textiles Ltd, who owes €10,460 is declared bankrupt, and the balance is written off as a bad debt.

General Journal

Date	Details	F	Dr €	Cr €
	To: i.e.	GL1 DL1		

20 A debtor, Pixel Printing Ltd, who owes €5,500 is declared bankrupt, and can only pay 20c in the €1. A cheque is received for this amount and the balance is written off as a bad debt.

General Journal

Date	Details	F	Dr €	Cr €
	Bank Bad debts To: Pixel Printing Ltd i.e.	CB GL1 DL1		

21 A debtor, Curtis & Co. Ltd, who owes Electrical Supplies Ltd €7,200 is declared bankrupt, and can only pay 25c in the €1. A cheque is received for this amount and the balance is written off as a bad debt.

General Journal (of Electrical Supplies Ltd)

Date	Details	F	Dr €	Cr €
	Bank Bad debts To: i.e.	CB GL1 DL1		

22 A debtor, Corrigan Ltd, who owes Building Supplies Ltd €25,000 is declared bankrupt, and can only pay 30c in the €1. A cheque is received for this amount and the balance is written off as a bad debt.

General Journal (of Building Supplies Ltd)

Date	Details	F	Dr €	Cr €
	To: i.e.	CB GL1 DL1		

23 A debtor, Select Ltd, who owes €42,000 is declared bankrupt, and can only pay 30c in the €1. A cheque is received for this amount and the balance is written off as a bad debt.

24 A debtor, Gorse Products Ltd, who owes €16,000 is declared bankrupt, and can only pay 40c in the €1. A cheque is received for this amount and the balance is written off as a bad debt.

25 A debtor, Computers Supplies Ltd, who owes Amos Computers €25,000 is declared bankrupt, and can only pay 10c in the €1. A cheque is received for this amount and the balance is written off as a bad debt.

Record each of the following 'uncommon entries' in the general journal and post to the relevant ledger accounts (using today's date).

26 On 31 December 2012 vehicles owned by Fastex Ltd valued at €65,000 are depreciated by 20%.

27 On 31/12/2013 machinery owned by Hult Engineering Ltd valued at €120,000 is depreciated by 20%.

28 On 31/12/2013 equipment owned by Montel & Co. Ltd valued at €24,000 is depreciated by 25%.

29 Explain the following terms.

(a) Depreciation: _____

_____

(b) Scrap value: _____

_____

(c) Straight line depreciation: _____

_____

30 On 1 January 2013 Brooke Ltd bought machinery by cheque for €35,000. Brooke Ltd estimate that the machinery will last for five years and have a scrap value of €5,000. Record the purchase of the machinery on 1 January 2013 and the annual depreciation written off for 2013 (31/12/2013) in the relevant books of first entry and in the relevant accounts.

31 On 1 January 2013 Moloney Wholesalers Ltd bought new delivery vans by cheque for €42,000 from Hinchy's Garage. Moloney Wholesalers Ltd estimate that the vans will last for six years and have a scrap value of €6,000. Record the purchase of the delivery vans on 1 January 2013 and the annual depreciation written off for 2013 (31/12/2013) in the relevant books of first entry and in the relevant accounts.

32 On 1 January 2013 Tierney Products Ltd bought new equipment by cheque for €78,000. Tierney Products Ltd estimate that the equipment will last five years and have a scrap value of €8,000. Record the purchase of the equipment on 1 January 2013 and the annual depreciation written off for 2013 (31/12/2013) and 2014 (31/12/2014) in the relevant books of first entry and in the relevant accounts.

Book-keeping Revision, Cash and Credit

1. The books of Long Ltd showed the following balances on 1 January 2013.

	€
Premises	240,000
Debtor: Rackett Ltd	11,000
Stock	49,000

(a) Enter these balances in the general journal, find the ordinary share capital balance, and post these balances to the relevant ledger accounts and analysed cash book.

(b) Post the relevant figures from the purchases book and the purchases returns book to the ledgers.

Purchases Day Book

Date 2013	Details	Invoice	F	Total € (excl. VAT)	VAT €	Total € (incl. VAT)
9 Jan	Browne Ltd	1	CL1	8,000	1,720	9,720
				8,000	1,720	9,720
				GL	GL	

Purchases Returns Day Book

Date 2013	Details	Credit note	F	Total € (excl. VAT)	VAT €	Total € (incl. VAT)
12 Jan	Browne Ltd	1	CL1	600	129	729
				GL	GL	

(c) Record the following bank transactions for the month of January. Post the relevant figures to the ledgers. Analyse the bank transactions under the following money column headings:
Debit (receipts) side: Bank; Sales; VAT; Debtors; Share Capital.
Credit (payments) side: Bank; Purchases; VAT; Creditors; Wages.

1/1/13	Shareholders invested €50,000 and this was lodged	
9/1/13	Cash sales, lodged	€26,730 (€22,000 + €4,730 VAT)
17/1/13	Rackett Ltd paid its account in full and this was lodged (receipt no. 1)	
19/1/13	Purchases for resale (cheque no. 1)	€11,000 + VAT @ 21.5%
23/1/13	Cash sales, lodged	€21,870 (€18,000 + €3,870 VAT)
28/1/13	Paid Browne Ltd, on account (cheque no. 2)	€6,000
29/1/13	Paid wages (cheque no. 3)	€9,600

(d) Balance the accounts on 31 January 2013, and extract a trial balance as at that date.

2 The books of Crean Ltd showed the following balances on 1 February 2013.

General Journal

Date 2013	Details	F	Debit €	Credit €
1 Feb	Furniture & fittings	GL1	75,000	
	Equipment	GL2	45,000	
	Stock	GL3	28,000	
	Bank	CB	12,000	
	Creditor: Creative Ltd a/c	CL1		10,000
	Ordinary share capital a/c	GL4		150,000
	Asset, liability & share capital of Crean Ltd		160,000	160,000

(a) Post the balances in the above general journal to the relevant ledger accounts.
(b) Post the relevant figures from the purchases book and the purchases returns book to the ledgers.

Purchases Day Book

Date 2013	Details	Invoice	F	Total € (excl. VAT)	VAT €	Total € (incl. VAT)
7 Feb	Creative Ltd	32	CL1	10,000	1,350	11,350
				GL	GL	

Purchases Returns Day Book

Date 2013	Details	Credit note	F	Total € (excl. VAT)	VAT €	Total € (incl. VAT)
10 Feb	Creative Ltd	9	CL1	400	54	454
				GL	GL	

(c) Record the following bank transactions for the month of February. Post the relevant figures to the ledgers.
Analyse the bank transactions under the following money column headings:
     Debit (receipts) side: Bank; Sales; VAT.
     Credit (payments) side: Bank; Purchases; VAT; Creditors; Insurance.

3/2/13	Paid insurance (cheque no. 19)	€6,400
13/2/13	Cash sales, lodged	€27,240 (€24,000 + €3,240 VAT)
22/2/13	Paid Creative Ltd in full (cheque no. 20)	
26/2/13	Purchases for resale (cheque no. 21)	€8,000 + VAT @ 13.5%
27/2/13	Cash sales, lodged	€22,700 (€20,000 + €2,700 VAT)

(d) Balance the accounts on 28 February 2013, and extract a trial balance as at that date.

3   The books of Hightower Ltd showed the following balances on 1 March 2013.

	€
Premises	330,000
Stock	26,000
Bank	10,000
Creditor: Saoil Ltd	16,000

(a) Enter these balances in the general journal, find the ordinary share capital balance and post these balances to the relevant ledger accounts.

(b) Post the relevant figures from the sales book and the purchases book to the ledgers.

Sales Day Book

Date 2013	Details	Invoice	F	Total € (excl. VAT)	VAT €	Total € (incl. VAT)
16 March	Windgate Ltd	31	DL1	9,000	1,215	10,215
				GL	GL	

Purchases Day Book

Date 2013	Details	Invoice	F	Total € (excl. VAT)	VAT €	Total € (incl. VAT)
10 March	Saoil Ltd	19	CL1	12,000	1,620	13,620
				GL	GL	

(c) Record the following bank transactions for the month of March. Post the relevant figures to the ledgers. Analyse the bank transactions under the following money column headings:

   Debit (receipts) side: Bank; Sales; VAT; Debtors.
   Credit (payments) side: Bank; Purchases; VAT; Creditors; Wages.

4/3/13	Cash sales, lodged	€17,025 (€15,000 + €2,025 VAT)
9/3/13	Paid wages (cheque no.1)	€7,250
16/3/13	Paid Saoil Ltd (cheque no. 2)	€15,000
19/3/13	Cash sales, lodged	€18,160 (€16,000 + €2,160 VAT)
20/3/13	Purchases for resale (cheque no. 3)	€8,000 + VAT @ 13.5%
23/3/13	Windgate Ltd paid its account in full and this was lodged (receipt no. 1)	

(d) Balance the accounts on 31 March 2013, and extract a trial balance as at that date.

4   The books of Saunders Ltd showed the following balances on 1 April 2013.

General Journal

Date 2013	Details	F	Debit €	Credit €
1 April	Plant & machinery	GL1	275,000	
	Vehicles	GL2	65,000	
	Furniture & fittings	GL3	45,000	
	Debtor: Landell Ltd a/c	DL1	21,000	
	Bank overdraft	CB		6,000
	Ordinary share capital a/c	GL4		400,000
	Assets, liabilities & share capital of Saunders Ltd		406,000	406,000

(a) Post the balances in the general journal to the relevant ledger accounts.

(b) Post the relevant figures from the sales book and the sales returns book to the ledgers.

Sales Day Book

Date 2013	Details	Invoice	F	Total € (excl. VAT)	VAT €	Total € (incl. VAT)
8 April	Landell Ltd	1	DL1	14,000	1,890	15,890
15 April	Price Ltd	2	DL2	16,000	2,160	18,160
				30,000	4,050	34,050
				GL	GL	

Sales Returns Day Book

Date 2013	Details	Credit note	F	Total € (excl. VAT)	VAT €	Total € (incl. VAT)
18 April	Price Ltd	1	DL2	1,000	135	1,135
				GL	GL	

(c) Record the following bank transactions for the month of April. Post the relevant figures to the ledgers. Analyse the bank transactions under the following money column headings:

   Debit (receipts) side: Bank; Sales; VAT; Debtors.
   Credit (payments) side: Bank; Purchases; VAT; Advertising.

5/4/13	Cash sales, lodged	€20,430 (€18,000 + €2,430 VAT)
9/4/13	Paid advertising (cheque no. 1)	€7,200
15/4/13	Landell Ltd paid its account in full and this was lodged (receipt no. 1)	
19/4/13	Cash sales, lodged	€17,025 (€15,000 + €2,025 VAT)
23/4/13	Price Ltd paid €9,000 and this was lodged (receipt no. 2)	
25/4/13	Purchases for resale (cheque no. 2)	€14,000 + VAT @ 13.5%

(d) Balance the accounts on 30 April 2013, and extract a trial balance as at that date.

5 The books of Baker Ltd showed the following balances on 1 May 2013.

	€
Equipment	82,000
Debtor: Woodpine Ltd	20,000
Stock	22,000
Bank	16,000

(a) Enter these balances in the general journal, find the ordinary share capital balance and post these balances to the relevant ledger accounts and analysed cash book.

(b) Post the relevant figures from the sales book and the sales returns book to the ledgers.

Sales Day Book

Date 2013	Details	Invoice	F	Total € (excl. VAT)	VAT €	Total € (incl. VAT)
6 May	Woodpine Ltd	11	DL1	20,000	4,300	24,300
18 May	Rover Ltd	12	DL2	30,000	6,450	36,450
				50,000	10,750	60,750
				GL	GL	

Sales Returns Day Book

Date 2013	Details	Credit note	F	Total € (excl. VAT)	VAT €	Total € (incl. VAT)
20 May	Rover Ltd	6	DL2	2,000	430	2,430
				GL	GL	

(c) Record the following bank transactions for the month of May. Post the relevant figures to the ledgers. Analyse the bank transactions under the following money column headings:

Debit (receipts) side: Bank; Sales; VAT; Debtors; Share Capital.
Credit (payments) side: Bank; Purchases; VAT; Insurance; Other.

5/5/13	Paid insurance (cheque no. 1)	€9,000
10/5/13	Cash sales, lodged	€38,880 (€32,000 + €6,880 VAT)
13/5/13	Purchases for resale (cheque no. 2)	€28,000 + VAT @ 21.5%
21/5/13	Woodpine Ltd paid its account in full and this was lodged (receipt no. 14)	
25/5/13	Shareholders invested €60,000 and this was lodged	
28/5/13	Rover Ltd paid, and this was lodged (receipt no. 15)	€20,000
30/5/13	Bought equipment (cheque no. 3)	€18,000

(d) Balance the accounts on 31 May 2013, and extract a trial balance as at that date.

6 The books of Largo Wholesalers Ltd showed the following balances on 1 January 2013.

General Journal

Date 2013	Details	F	Debit €	Credit €
1 Jan	Premises	GL1	290,000	
	Vehicles	GL2	74,000	
	Stock	GL3	42,000	
	Bank	CB	20,000	
	Creditor: Orwell Ltd a/c	CL1		26,000
	Ordinary share capital a/c	GL4		400,000
	Assets, liabilities & share capital of Largo Wholesalers Ltd		426,000	426,000

(a) Post the balances in the above general journal to the relevant ledger accounts.
(b) Post the relevant figures from the purchases book and the purchases returns book to the ledgers.

Purchases Day Book

Date 2013	Details	Invoice	F	Total € (excl. VAT)	VAT €	Total € (incl. VAT)
8 Jan	Orwell Ltd	3	CL1	20,000	2,700	22,700
16 Jan	Trent Ltd	8	CL2	24,000	3,240	27,240
				44,000	5,940	49,940
				GL	GL	

Purchases Returns Day Book

Date 2013	Details	Credit note	F	Total € (excl. VAT)	VAT €	Total € (incl. VAT)
18 Jan	Trent Ltd	1	CL2	3,200	432	3,632
				GL	GL	

(c) Record the following bank transactions for the month of January. Post the relevant figures to the ledgers. Analyse the bank transactions under the following money column headings:

Debit (receipts) side: Bank; Sales; VAT.
Credit (payments) side: Bank; Purchases; VAT; Creditor; Wages; Other.

4/1/13	Purchases for resale (cheque no. 1)	€15,000 + VAT @ 13.5%
8/1/13	Cash sales, lodged	€68,100 (€60,000 + €8,100 VAT)
13/1/13	Paid Orwell Ltd (cheque no. 2)	€35,000
22/1/13	Cash sales, lodged	€49,940 (€44,000 + €5,940 VAT)
25/1/13	Bought a vehicle (cheque no. 3)	€22,000
26/1/13	Paid Trent Ltd in full settlement (cheque no. 4)	
30/1/13	Paid wages (cheque no. 5)	€14,000

(d) Balance the accounts on 31 January 2013, and extract a trial balance as at that date.

7 The books of Print Supplies Ltd showed the following balances on 1 February 2013.

	€
Premises	520,000
Equipment	54,000
Creditor: Dixon Ltd	24,000

(a) Enter these balances in the general journal, find the ordinary share capital balance and post these balances to the relevant ledger accounts.
(b) Post the relevant figures from the sales book and the purchases book to the ledgers.

Sales Day Book

Date 2013	Details	Invoice	F	Total € (excl. VAT)	VAT €	Total € (incl. VAT)
6 Feb	Design Print Ltd	36	DL1	24,000	3,240	27,240
				GL	GL	

Purchases Day Book

Date 2013	Details	Invoice	F	Total € (excl. VAT)	VAT €	Total € (incl. VAT)
9 Feb	Dixon Ltd	19	CL1	17,000	2,295	19,295
				GL	GL	

(c) Record the following bank transactions for the month of February. Post the relevant figures to the ledgers. Analyse the bank transactions under the following money column headings:

Debit (receipts) side: Bank; Sales; VAT; Debtors.
Credit (payments) side: Bank; Purchases; VAT; Creditors; Advertising; Wages.

6/2/13	Cash sales, lodged	€35,185 (€31,000 + €4,185 VAT)
10/2/13	Paid advertising (cheque no. 21)	€8,400
15/2/13	Paid Dixon Ltd (cheque no. 22)	€25,000
20/2/13	Cash sales, lodged	€24,970 (€22,000 + €2,970 VAT)
22/2/13	Purchases for resale (cheque no. 23)	€19,000 + VAT @ 13.5%
25/2/13	Design Print Ltd paid its account in full and this was lodged (receipt no. 9)	
28/2/13	Paid wages (cheque no. 24)	€9,840

(d) Balance the accounts on 28 February 2013, and extract a trial balance as at that date.

8   The books of H.G. Wells Ltd showed the following balances on 1 March 2013.

General Journal

Date 2013	Details	F	Dr €	Cr €
1 March	Equipment	GL1	120,000	
	Vehicles	GL2	54,000	
	Stock	GL3	28,000	
	Bank	CB	26,000	
	Debtor: Connolly Ltd a/c	DL1	12,000	
	Ordinary share capital a/c	GL4		240,000
	Assets, liabilities & share capital of H.G. Wells Ltd		240,000	240,000

(a) Post the balances in the above general journal to the relevant ledger accounts.
(b) Post the relevant figures from the sales book and the purchases book to the ledgers.

Purchases Day Book

Date 2013	Details	Invoice	F	Total € (excl. VAT)	VAT €	Total € (incl. VAT)
8 March	Booker Ltd	132	CL1	30,000	6,450	36,450
				GL	GL	

Sales Day Book

Date 2013	Details	Invoice	F	Total € (excl. VAT)	VAT €	Total € (incl. VAT)
12 March	Forbes Ltd	98	DL1	45,000	9,675	54,675
				GL	GL	

(c) Record the following bank transactions for the month of March. Post the relevant figures to the ledgers. Analyse the bank transactions under the following money column headings:

Debit (receipts) side: Bank; Sales; VAT; Debtors.
Credit (payments) side: Bank; Purchases; VAT; Creditors; Insurance.

5/3/13	Cash sales, lodged	€72,900 (€60,000 + €12,900 VAT)
10/3/13	Paid insurance (cheque no. 1)	€15,600
15/3/13	Paid Booker Ltd (cheque no. 2), in full settlement	
19/3/13	Cash sales, lodged	€51,030 (€42,000 + €9,030 VAT)
21/3/13	Purchases for resale (cheque no. 3)	€45,000 + VAT @ 21.5%
25/3/13	Connolly Ltd paid its account in full and this was lodged (receipt no. 1)	
28/3/13	Forbes Ltd paid, and this was lodged (receipt no. 2)	€40,000

(d) Balance the accounts on 31 March 2013, and extract a trial balance as at that date.

9 The books of Lisgo Ltd showed the following balances on 1 April 2013.

General Journal

Date 2013	Details	F	Debit €	Credit €
1 April	Premises	GL1	550,000	
	Vehicles	GL2	72,000	
	Furniture & fittings	GL3	36,000	
	Equipment	GL4	31,000	
	Debtor: Principles Ltd a/c	DL1	18,000	
	Bank overdraft	CB		7,000
	Ordinary share capital a/c	GL5		700,000
	Assets, liabilities & share capital Lisgo Ltd		707,000	707,000

(a) Post the balances in the above general journal to the relevant ledger accounts.
(b) Post the relevant figures from the sales book and the sales returns book to the ledgers.

Sales Day Book

Date 2013	Details	Invoice	F	Total € (excl. VAT)	VAT €	Total € (incl. VAT)
10 April	Principles Ltd	11	DL1	12,000	1,620	13,620
18 April	Roxy Ltd	12	DL2	14,000	1,890	15,890
				26,000	3,510	29,510
				GL	GL	

Sales Returns Day Book

Date 2013	Details	Credit note	F	Total € (excl. VAT)	VAT €	Total € (incl. VAT)
12 April	Principles Ltd	5	DL1	1,200	162	1,362
21 April	Roxy Ltd	9	DL2	800	108	908
				2,000	270	2,270
				GL	GL	

(c) Record the following bank transactions for the month of April. Post the relevant figures to the ledgers. Analyse the bank transactions under the following money column headings:

Debit (receipts) side: Bank; Sales; VAT; Debtors.

Credit (payments) side: Bank; Purchases; VAT; Insurance; Wages.

7/4/13	Cash sales, lodged	€18,387 (€16,200 + €2,187 VAT)
10/4/13	Paid insurance (cheque no. 20)	€7,900
15/4/13	Principles Ltd paid its account in full and this was lodged (receipt no. 7)	
22/4/13	Cash sales, lodged	€12,485 (€11,000 + €1,485 VAT)
23/4/13	Roxy Ltd paid €8,500 and this was lodged (receipt no. 8)	
26/4/13	Purchases for resale (cheque no. 21)	€17,000 + VAT @ 13.5%
29/4/13	Paid wages (cheque no. 22)	€7,400

(d) Balance the accounts on 30 April 2013, and extract a trial balance as at that date.

10 The following transactions took place during the month of January 2013.

Credit Transactions

Date	Details	No.	€
4/1/13	Purchased goods on credit from Bracken & Co. Ltd	Invoice 2	16,000 + VAT @ 13.5%
7/1/13	Returned goods to Bracken & Co. Ltd (unordered)	Credit note 1	2,000 + VAT @ 13.5%
21/1/13	Sold goods on credit to Murray Ltd	Invoice 1	34,000 + VAT @ 13.5%

Cash Transactions

Date	Details	€
2/1/13	Shareholders invest €250,000 and this was lodged	
8/1/13	Purchases for resale (cheque no. 1)	8,000 + VAT @ 13.5%
14/1/13	Paid expenses (cheque no. 2)	4,300
26/1/13	Murray Ltd paid on account and this was lodged (receipt no. 1)	25,000
27/1/13	Paid Bracken & Co. Ltd its account in full (cheque no. 3)	

(a) Record the transactions for the month of January 2013 in the appropriate books of first entry. Post the relevant figures to the ledgers. Analyse the bank transactions under the following money column headings:

Debit (receipts) side: Bank; Sales; VAT; Debtors; Share Capital.

Credit (payments) side: Bank; Purchases; VAT; Creditors; Expenses.

(b) Balance the accounts on 31 January 2013, and extract a trial balance as at that date.

11 Pine Furniture Ltd had the following balances in its general journal on 1 February 2013.

General Journal

Date 2013	Details	F	Debit €	Credit €
1 Feb	Premises	GL1	360,000	
	Motor vans	GL2	48,000	
	Equipment	GL3	24,000	
	Bank	CB	19,000	
	Debtor: Hannon Ltd a/c	DL1	17,000	
	Creditor: Timber Products Ltd	CL1		18,000
	Ordinary share capital a/c	GL4		450,000
	Assets, liabilities & share capital Pine Furniture Ltd		468,000	468,000

(a) Post the balances in the above general journal to the relevant ledger accounts.

The following transactions took place during the month of February 2013.

Credit Transactions

Date	Details	Invoice No.	€
6/2/13	Purchased goods on credit from Timber Products Ltd	42	24,000 + VAT @ 13.5%
10/2/13	Sold goods on credit to Casey's Ltd	27	22,000 + VAT @ 13.5%
21/2/13	Sold goods on credit to Hannon Ltd	28	13,000 + VAT @ 13.5%

Cash Transactions

Date	Details	€
8/2/13	Cash sales, lodged	10,442 (9,200 + 1,242 VAT)
11/2/13	Paid wages (cheque no. 1)	5,800
16/2/13	Purchased goods for resale (cheque no. 2)	8,000 + VAT @ 13.5%
21/2/13	Hannon Ltd settled in full and this was lodged (receipt no. 1)	
26/2/13	Paid Timber Products Ltd (cheque no. 3)	35,000
28/2/13	Received a cheque, lodged, from Casey's Ltd (receipt no. 2)	13,000

(b) Record the transactions for the month of February 2013 in the appropriate books of first entry. Post the relevant figures to the ledgers. Analyse the bank transactions under the following money column headings:
   Debit (receipts) side: Bank; Sales; VAT; Debtors.
   Credit (payments) side: Bank; Purchases; VAT; Creditors; Wages.

(c) Balance the accounts on 28 February 2013, and extract a trial balance as at that date.

12 O'Reillys Ltd had the following balances in its general journal on 1 March 2013.

General Journal

Date 2013	Details	F	Debit €	Credit €
1 March	Premises	GL1	510,000	
	Motor vans	GL2	38,000	
	Equipment	GL3	47,000	
	Stock	GL4	20,000	
	Debtor: Roberts Ltd a/c	DL1	21,000	
	Bank overdraft	CB		11,000
	Creditors: Turbridy Ltd	CL1		25,000
	Ordinary share capital a/c	GL5		600,000
	Assets, liabilities & share capital of O'Reillys Ltd		636,000	636,000

(a) Post the balances in the above general journal to the relevant ledger accounts.

The following transactions took place during the month of March 2013.

Credit Transactions

Date	Details	Invoice No.	€
5/3/13	Purchased goods on credit Turbridy Ltd	74	11,000 + VAT @ 21.5%
9/3/13	Sold goods on credit to Roberts Ltd	102	14,000 + VAT @ 21.5%
19/3/13	Sold goods on credit to Hickey & Co. Ltd	103	13,000 + VAT @ 21.5%
27/3/13	Bought a van, for business use, on credit from Trucksales Ltd	21	14,200 + VAT @ 21.5%

Cash Transactions

Date	Details	€
3/3/13	Cash sales, lodged	19,440 (16,000 + 3,440 VAT)
7/3/13	Paid insurance (cheque no. 1)	4,700
15/3/13	Roberts Ltd settled in full and this was lodged (receipt no. 1)	
16/3/13	Purchased goods for resale (cheque no. 2)	17,000 + VAT @ 21.5%
19/3/13	Cash sales, lodged	12,150 (10,000 + 2,150 VAT)
22/3/13	Paid Turbridy Ltd (cheque no. 3)	26,000
26/3/13	Hickey & Co. Ltd paid in full settlement (receipt no. 2)	
29/3/13	Paid Trucksales Ltd (cheque no. 4)	550

(b) Record the transactions for the month of March 2013 in the appropriate books of first entry. Post the relevant figures to the ledgers. Analyse the bank transactions under the following money column headings:
   Debit (receipts) side: Bank; Sales; VAT; Debtors.
   Credit (payments) side: Bank; Purchases; VAT; Creditors; Insurance.

(c) Balance the accounts on 31 March 2013, and extract a trial balance as at that date.

Trading Account

1 Match the following terms with the appropriate definitions.

1	Trading account	A	Summary of assets and liabilities.
2	Profit & loss account	B	Some profit given as dividends and the balance retained.
3	Appropriation account	C	To find the net profit after expenses are paid.
4	Balance sheet	D	To find the gross profit.

1	2	3	4

2 Find the gross profit in each of the following cases.

(a)	€	**(b)**	€	**(c)**	€
Sales	= 180,000	Sales	= 635,000	Sales	= 96,000
Purchases	= 105,000	Purchases	= 347,000	Purchases	= 67,000
Gross profit		Gross profit		Gross profit	

(d)	€	**(e)**	€	**(f)**	€
Sales	= 1,940,000	Sales	= 810,000	Sales	= 516,700
Purchases	= 1,105,000	Purchases	= 496,000	Purchases	= 327,850
Gross profit		Gross profit		Gross profit	

3 Explain the following terms.

(a) Purchases returns: _A good that you brought that you brought it back because it could have been faulty._

(b) Sales returns: _A good that someone bought from you that they have brought back_

4 Complete the following trading account and find the gross profit.

Trading Account for year ended 31/12/2013

	€	€	€
Sales		804,000	
Less sales returns		12,000	
Net sales			
Less cost of sales:			
Purchases		492,000	
Less purchases returns		8,000	
Cost of sales			
Gross profit			

5 Complete the following trading account and find the gross profit.

Trading Account for year ended 31/12/2013

	€	€	€
Sales		680,000	
Less sales returns		7,600	
Net sales			
Less cost of sales:			
Purchases		402,000	
Less purchases returns		9,000	
Cost of sales			
Gross profit			

6 Complete the following trading account and find the gross profit.

Trading Account for year ended 31/12/2013

	€	€	€
Sales		945,720	
Less sales returns		14,650	
Net sales			
Less cost of sales:			
Purchases		516,650	
Less purchases returns		17,400	
Cost of sales			
Gross profit			

7 Complete the following trading account and find the gross profit.

Trading Account for year ended 31/12/2013

	€	€	€
Sales		364,840	
Less sales returns		8,900	
Net sales			
Less cost of sales:			
Purchases		246,350	
Less purchases returns		7,420	
Cost of sales			
Gross profit			

8 Complete the following trading account and find the gross profit.

Trading Account for year ended 31/12/2013

	€	€	€
Sales		524,600	
Less sales returns		9,800	
Net sales			
Less cost of sales:			
Opening stock (1/1/13)		17,400	
Purchases	306,720		
Less purchases returns	11,250		
Cost of sales			
Gross profit			

9 Complete the following trading account and find the gross profit.

Trading Account for year ended 31/12/2013

	€	€	€
Sales		226,940	
Less sales returns		6,220	
Net sales			
Less cost of sales:			
Opening stock (1/1/13)		11,800	
Purchases	134,840		
Less purchases returns	9,360		
Cost of sales			
Gross profit			

10 Complete the following trading account and find the gross profit.

Trading Account for year ended 31/12/2013

	€	€	€
Sales		789,740	
Less sales returns		15,820	
Net sales			*595,920*
Less cost of sales:			
Opening stock (1/1/13)		23,600	
Purchases	398,420		
Less purchases returns	14,360	*384,060*	
Cost of sales			
Gross profit			

11 Complete the following trading account and find the gross profit.

Trading Account for year ended 31/12/2013

	€	€	€
Sales		682,350	
Less sales returns		14,600	
Net sales			667750
Less cost of sales:			
Opening stock (1/1/13)		25,700	
Purchases	374,480		
Less purchases returns	10,580	363,900	
		389600	
Closing stock (31/12/13)		22,400	
Cost of sales			367200
Gross profit			300550

12 Complete the following trading account and find the gross profit.

Trading Account for year ended 31/12/2013

	€	€	€
Sales		481,430	
Less sales returns		6,700	
Net sales			474730
Less cost of sales:			
Opening stock (1/1/13)		16,450	
Purchases	265,200		
Less purchases returns	5,750	259450	
		275900	
Closing stock (31/12/13)		15,300	
Cost of goods sold			260,600
Gross profit			214,130

13 Complete the following trading account and find the gross profit.

Trading Account for year ended 31/12/2013

	€	€	€
Sales		718,650	
Less sales returns		13,900	
Net sales			704750
Less cost of sales:			
Opening stock (1/1/13)		21,600	
Purchases	364,970		
Less purchases returns	9,820	355150	
		376750	
Closing stock (31/12/13)		23,150	
Cost of sales			353,600
Gross profit			351,150

14 Complete the following trading account and find the gross profit.

Trading Account for year ended 31/12/2013

	€	€	€
Sales		348,240	
Less sales returns		11,750	
Net sales			336490
Less cost of sales:			
Opening stock (1/1/13)		14,760	
Purchases	186,800		
Less purchases returns	7,640	179,160	
		193,920	
Closing stock (31/12/13)		13,330	
Cost of sales			180590
Gross profit			155900

15 Prepare a trading account for year ended 31/12/2012.
Stock (1/1/2012) €31,500; Purchases €738,000; Sales €1,640,000; Purchases returns €16,750; Sales returns €21,720; Stock (31/12/2012) €33,350.

16 Prepare a trading account for year ended 31/10/2013.
Stock (1/1/2013) €19,400; Purchases €428,000; Sales €656,400; Purchases returns €7,800; Sales returns €8,600; Stock (31/12/2013) €20,900.

17 Prepare a trading account for year ended 31/12/2013.
Stock (1/1/2013) €38,000; Purchases €856,000; Sales €1,755,000; Purchases returns €18,200; Sales returns €21,800; Stock (30/12/2013) €36,400.

18 Prepare a trading account for year ended 31/12/2013.
Stock (1/1/2013) €16,600; Purchases €578,800; Sales €921,650; Purchases returns €9,300; Sales returns €12,300; Stock (31/12/2013) €20,100; Carriage inwards €4,150.

19 Prepare a trading account for Bell Tech Ltd for year ended 31/12/2013.
Stock (1/1/2013) €30,800; Purchases €617,500; Sales €1,376,550; Purchases returns €7,000; Sales returns €13,450; Stock (31/12/2013) €28,300; Carriage inwards €9,800; Customs duty €58,000.

20 Prepare a trading account for Turner & Co. Ltd for year ended 31/12/2013.
Stock (1/1/2013) €24,200; Purchases €589,500; Sales €1,108,080; Purchases returns €11,200; Sales returns €13,580; Stock (31/12/2013) €26,500; Customs duty €62,400.

21 Prepare a trading account for Flexron Ltd for year ended 31/12/2013.
Purchases €482,600; Sales €986,450; Purchases returns €6,200; Sales returns €9,150; Stock (31/12/2013) €19,200; Carriage inwards €10,800; Manufacturing wages €93,600; Stock (1/1/2013) €18,400.

22 **(a)** Stock is normally valued at the lowest of three possible prices. Name the three possible prices.

(i) _____

(ii) _____

(iii) _____

(b) Give two reasons why stocktaking should be carried out.

(i) _____

_____

(ii) _____

_____

23 **(a)** Explain the procedure for undertaking stocktaking. _____

_____

_____

_____

_____

(b) Explain how information technology can assist in stocktaking. Give two benefits of its use.

_____

_____

_____

Benefits: **(i)** _____

(ii) _____

24 **(a)** Close off these accounts to the trading account on 31/12/2013.
(b) Prepare a trading account for the year ending 31/12/2013.

Dr   General Ledger   Cr

2013	Details	F	Total	2013	Details	F	Total
Purchases A/C [1]							
31/12	Balance	b/d	124,800				
Sales A/C [2]							
				31/12	Balance	b/d	276,400
Stock A/C [3]							
1/1	Balance	b/d	13,800				
31/12	Balance	b/d	11,650				
Sales Returns A/C [4]							
31/12	Balance	b/d	9,100				
Purchases Returns A/C [5]							
				31/12	Balance	b/d	6,200

25 **(a)** Close off these accounts to the trading account on 31/12/2013.
(b) Prepare a trading account for the year ending 31/12/2013.

Dr   General Ledger   Cr

2013	Details	F	Total	2013	Details	F	Total
Purchases A/C [1]							
31/12	Balance	b/d	410,340				
Sales A/C [2]							
				31/12	Balance	b/d	774,060
Stock A/C [3]							
1/1	Balance	b/d	26,460				
31/12	Balance	b/d	24,885				
Sales Returns A/C [4]							
31/12	Balance	b/d	15,435				
Carriage Inwards A/C [5]							
31/12	Balance	b/d	14,910				
Purchases Returns A/C [6]							
				31/12	Balance	b/d	10,080

Profit and Loss Account

1 Find the net profit or loss in each of the following cases.

(a)   **€**
Gross profit = 457,800
Expenses   = 305,200

Net profit _____

(b)   **€**
Gross profit = 1,156,500
Expenses   = 829,650

Net profit _____

(c)   **€**
Gross profit = 143,260
Expenses   = 127,480

Net profit _____

(d)   **€**
Gross profit = 978,000
Expenses   = 1,004,500

Net loss _____

(e)   **€**
Gross profit = 874,320
Expenses   = 548,790

Net profit _____

(f)   **€**
Gross profit = 636,430
Expenses   = 871,550

Net loss _____

2 Explain each of the following terms.

(a) Carriage outwards: _____

_____

(b) Additional gains: _____

_____

(c) Net profit: _____

_____

3 Complete the following profit and loss account and find the net profit.

Profit and Loss Account for year ended 31/12/2013

	€	€	€
Gross profit			524,870
Less expenses:			
Rent		36,000	
Wages		128,000	
Insurance		10,500	
Advertising		15,800	
General expenses		22,320	
Net profit			

4 Complete the following profit and loss account and find the net profit.

Profit and Loss Account for year ended 31/12/2013

	€	€	€
Gross profit			298,520
Less expenses:			
Rent & rates		38,000	
Wages		116,400	
Insurance		8,100	
Light & heat		9,460	
General expenses		14,180	
Net profit			

5 Complete the following profit and loss account and find the net profit/loss.

Profit and Loss Account for year ended 31/12/2013

	€	€	€
Gross profit			819,670
Interest received			860
Less expenses:			
Rent & rates		52,600	
Wages & salaries		346,780	
Insurance		14,640	
Light & heat		23,220	
Bad debts		18,650	
General expenses		19,740	
Net profit			

6 Complete the following profit and loss account and find the net profit/loss.

Profit and Loss Account for year ended 31/12/2013

	€	€	€
Gross profit			454,300
Less expenses:			
Rent & rates		48,000	
Wages & salaries		305,000	
Advertising		26,400	
Light & heat		21,850	
Bad debts		38,200	
General expenses		24,430	
Net profit			

7 Explain each of the following terms.

(a) Bad debts: _____

_____

(b) Commission received: _____

_____

8 Complete the following profit and loss account and find the net profit/loss.

Profit and Loss Account for year ended 31/12/2013

	€	€	€
Gross profit			643,720
Rent received			7,200
Less expenses:			
Wages & salaries		292,240	
Insurance		12,560	
Light & heat		16,200	
Bad debts		11,000	
Carriage out		32,400	
General expenses		14,820	
Net profit			

9 Prepare a profit and loss account for Largesse Ltd for the year ended 31/12/2013.

Gross profit	€777,000
Wages & salaries	€309,000
Insurance	€21,600
Heat & light	€11,200
Advertising	€43,500
Telephone/Internet	€5,100
Bad debts	€16,100
Rent & rates	€33,800
General expenses	€15,200
Bank charges & interest	€840
Carriage out	€23,700

10   Prepare a profit and loss account for Celtic Resources Ltd for the year ended 31/12/2013.

Gross profit		€366,240
Wages & salaries	€198,744	
Insurance	€11,520	
Heat & light	€8,750	
Advertising	€24,000	
Telephone/Internet	€5,200	
Commission	€15,600	
Bad debts	€10,150	
Rent & rates	€49,000	
General expenses	€16,800	
Bank charges & interest	€1,070	
Carriage out	€29,640	

11   Prepare a profit and loss account for Shamrock Ltd for the year ended 31/12/2013.

Gross profit		€1,468,000
Rent received		€20,800
Wages & salaries	€618,000	
Insurance	€23,480	
Heat & light	€16,700	
Advertising	€52,000	
Telephone/Internet	€7,800	
Interest received		€1,200
Bad debts	€9,250	
Rates	€18,400	
General expenses	€28,600	
Carriage out	€44,570	

12   Prepare a profit and loss account for the year ended 31/12/2013.
Gross profit €493,800; Wages €288,100; Insurance €14,200; Telephone/Internet €8,320; Mortgage repayments €54,600; Discount received €14,000; Heat & light €8,640; Carriage out €46,600; General expenses €15,350; Advertising €35,000; Rates €10,000.

13   Prepare a profit and loss account for the year ended 31/12/2013.
Gross profit €282,810; Wages €168,000; Telephone/Internet €7,280; Rent & rates €46,200; Commission received €9,600; Heat & light €12,800; Carriage out €42,900; General expenses €13,200; Insurance €15,720; Advertising €32,000.

14   Explain each of the following terms.

(a) Revenue expenditure: _____

_____

(b) Capital expenditure: _____

_____

15   Tick the appropriate box (✔) to show whether the following items would be classified as revenue or capital expenditure for a retail hardware business.

	Revenue expenditure	Capital expenditure
Purchase of stock for resale.		
Extension to the premises.		
Purchase of a new delivery truck.		
Paid for insurance.		

16   The following trial balance was extracted from the books of Rock Ltd on 31 December 2013. Prepare the company's trading A/C and profit and loss A/C for the year ended 31/12/2013.

	Dr	Cr
	€	€
Purchases & sales	364,000	756,000
Stock (1/1/2013)	25,200	
Purchases returns		7,840
Insurance	13,440	
Heat & light	21,840	
Interest received		1,792
Sales returns	8,960	
Carriage in	5,600	
Carriage out	12,600	
Salaries	193,200	
Telephone/Internet	5,040	
Rent	29,120	

Note: closing stock (31/12/2013) = €28,700.

17   The following trial balance was extracted from the books of Primary Ltd on 31 December 2013. Prepare the company's trading A/C and profit and loss A/C for the year ended 31/12/2013.

	Dr	Cr
	€	€
Purchases & sales	555,360	982,320
Stock (1/1/2013)	29,760	
Purchases returns		9,120
Sales returns	11,100	
Rent & rates	45,600	
Insurance	19,440	
Heat & light	18,600	
Commission received		13,800
Advertising	12,240	
Discount received		6,500
Carriage in	13,080	
Customs duty	27,760	
Carriage out	19,680	
Wages & salaries	161,760	
Telephone	17,760	
Bank charges & interest	1,750	

Note: closing stock (31/12/2013) = €26,100.

18 Tick the appropriate box (✔) to show whether the following items would be classified as revenue or capital expenditure for a retail business.

	Revenue expenditure	Capital expenditure
Purchase of equipment for business use.		
Payment of wages.		
Paid advertising.		
Bought a display cabinet.		

19 The following trial balance was extracted from the books of Greenway Ltd on 31 December 2013. Prepare the company's trading A/C and profit and loss A/C for the year ended 31/12/2013.

	Dr	Cr
	€	€
Purchases & sales	391,000	748,000
Stock (1/1/2013)	18,700	
Purchases returns		7,650
Advertising	27,000	
Heat & light	20,100	
Rent received		19,950
Sales returns	11,560	
Carriage in	6,800	
Carriage out	14,280	
Wages & salaries	156,400	
Telephone/Internet	15,470	
Rent & rates	21,420	

Note: closing stock (31/12/2013) = €20,700.

20 The following trial balance was extracted from the books of Meehans Ltd on 31 December 2013. Prepare the company's trading A/C and profit and loss A/C for the year ended 31/12/2013.

	Dr	Cr
	€	€
Purchases & sales	840,000	1,465,600
Stock (1/1/2013)	25,200	
Purchases returns		16,800
Sales returns	6,200	
Telephone/Internet	8,850	
Bank charges	525	
Heat & light	13,200	
Discount received		8,400
Office expenses	2,350	
Insurance	11,750	
Bad debts	9,225	
Customs duty	44,700	
Carriage out	24,000	
Wages & salaries	174,500	
Rent & rates	28,200	

Note: closing stock (31/12/2013) = €27,100.

21 Prepare the company's trading A/C and profit and loss A/C for the year ended 31/12/2013.

Dr   **General Ledger**   **Cr**

2013	Details	F	Total	2013	Details	F	Total
			Purchases A/C [1]				
31/12	Balance	b/d	576,000				
			Purchases Returns A/C				
				31/12	Balance	b/d	9,000
			Stock A/C				
1/01	Balance	b/d	24,500				
31/12	Balance	b/d	26,200				
			Carriage Inwards A/C				
31/12	Balance	b/d	11,500				
			Insurance A/C				
31/12	Balance	b/d	18,500				
			Carriage Outwards A/C				
31/12	Balance	b/d	24,000				
			Telephone A/C				
31/12	Balance	b/d	8,400				

Dr   **General Ledger**   **Cr**

2013	Details	F	Total	2013	Details	F	Total
			Sales A/C				
				31/12	Balance	b/d	970,000
			Sales Returns A/C				
31/12	Balance	b/d	14,200				
			Customs Duty A/C				
31/12	Balance	b/d	38,000				
			Wages A/C				
31/12	Balance	b/d	129,000				
			Heat & Light A/C				
31/12	Balance	b/d	17,400				
			Advertising A/C				
31/12	Balance	b/d	45,000				
			Discount Received A/C				
				31/12	Balance	b/d	6,800
			Rent A/C				
				31/12	Balance	b/d	28,000

Profit and Loss Appropriation Account

1 Explain the following terms.

(a) Dividend: _____

_____

(b) Retained earnings: _____

_____

2 Give two advantages of using retained earnings as a source of finance.

(a) _____

_____

(b) _____

_____

Calculate the reserves ('retained earnings') in each of the following cases.

3 Net profit = €235,500   Dividend = €150,000   Reserves = €_____

4 Net profit = €1,420,000   Dividend = €900,000   Reserves = €_____

5 Net profit = €867,000   Dividend = €600,000   Reserves = €_____

Calculate the total dividend in each of the following.

6 Issued share capital is €500,000. Declared dividend is 15%.   Dividend = €_____

7 Issued share capital is €200,000. Dividend declared is 20%.   Dividend = €_____

8 Issued share capital is €600,000. Declared dividend is 12%.   Dividend = €_____

9 Authorised share capital is €1 million. Issued share capital is €400,000. Proposed dividend is 12.5%.

Dividend = €_____

10 Authorised share capital is €10 million. Issued share capital is €2,500,000. Proposed dividend is 10%.

Dividend = €_____

11 Complete the following profit and loss appropriation account.

Profit and Loss Appropriation Account
for year ended 31/12/2013

	€	€	€
Net profit			264,500
Dividend			
Revenue reserve			

Dividend paid = €150,000.

12 Complete the following profit and loss appropriation account.

Profit and Loss Appropriation Account
for year ended 31/12/2013

	€	€	€
Net profit			746,850
Dividend			
Revenue reserve			

Dividend paid = €425,000.

13 Complete the following profit and loss appropriation account.

Profit and Loss Appropriation Account
for year ended 31/12/2013

	€	€	€
Net profit			61,360
Dividend			
Revenue reserve			

Issued share capital = €300,000.
Dividend declared = 8%.

14 Complete the following profit and loss appropriation account.

Profit and Loss Appropriation Account
for year ended 31/12/2013

	€	€	€
Net profit			384,660
Dividend			
Revenue reserve			

Issued share capital = €2,000,000.
Dividend declared = 12%.

15 Complete the following profit and loss appropriation account.

Profit and Loss Appropriation Account
for year ended 31/12/2013

	€	€	€
Net profit			240,000
Dividend			
Revenue reserve			

Issued share capital = €3,000,000.
Dividend declared = 5%.

16 Prepare a profit and loss appropriation account (year ended 31/12/2013) from the following.
Net profit is €346,750. Authorised share capital is 2,000,000 ordinary shares @ €1 each. Issued share capital is €1,200,000. Declared dividend is 15%.

17 Prepare a profit and loss appropriation account (year ended 31/12/2013) from the following.
Net profit is €570,000. Authorised share capital is 5,000,000 ordinary shares @ €1 each. Issued share capital is €2,600,000. Declared dividend is 12.5%.

18 Prepare a profit and loss appropriation account (year ended 31/12/2013) from the following.
Net profit is €97,500. Authorised share capital is 1,000,000 ordinary shares @ €1 each. Issued share capital is €600,000. Declared dividend is 12%. Profit and loss balance (reserves) €36,000.

19 Prepare a profit and loss appropriation account (year ended 31/12/2013) from the following.
Net profit is €138,800. Authorised share capital is 2,000,000 ordinary shares @ €1 each. Issued share capital = €900,000. Declared dividend is 10%. Profit and loss balance (reserves) €116,500.

20 Calculate the dividend that a shareholder will receive in each of the following cases.
Authorised share capital is €500,000. Issued share capital is €300,000.
Net profit is €72,000. Proposed dividend is 15%. (€1 ordinary shares.)
(a) 200 shares; **(b)** 1,500 shares; **(c)** 40,000 shares.

21 Calculate the dividend that a shareholder will receive in each of the following cases.
Authorised share capital is €2,000,000. Issued share capital is €800,000.
Net profit is €110,000. Proposed dividend is 8%. (€1 ordinary shares.)
(a) 150 shares;　　　**(b)** 9,000 shares;　　　**(c)** 80,000 shares.

22 Authorised share capital = €1,000,000 ordinary shares (€1). Net profit = €90,000.
Issued share capital = €600,000. Dividend paid = €72,000.
Tick (✔) which of the following figures is the percentage dividend paid.

7.2%		8%		12%		15%	

23 The following trial balance was extracted from the books of Retrograde Ltd on 31 December 2013. Prepare the trading, profit and loss and appropriation accounts for the year to date. The authorised share capital is 750,000 €1 ordinary shares.

	Dr	Cr
Purchases and sales	424,000	816,000
Sales returns and purchases returns	24,000	14,400
Bad debts	10,400	
Insurance	16,000	
Rent receivable		22,720
Carriage inwards	16,960	
Opening stock (1/1/2013)	40,000	
Wages and salaries	131,200	
Bank interest	2,200	
Advertising	25,600	
Issued share capital: 500,000 €1 shares		500,000

You are given the following additional information on 31/12/2013: (a) Closing stock €44,800. (b) Dividend declared 10%.

24 The following trial balance was extracted from the books of Trident Ltd on 31 December 2013. You are required to prepare the trading, profit and loss and appropriation accounts for the year ended 31/12/2013. The authorised share capital is 500,000 €1 ordinary shares.

	Dr	Cr
Purchases and sales	360,000	820,000
Sales returns and purchases returns	6,000	
Carriage outwards	14,500	
Commission receivable		12,000
Advertising	40,000	
Opening stock (1/1/2013)	34,000	
Carriage inwards	8,200	
Wages and salaries	226,000	
Light and heat	9,400	
Import duty on purchases	36,000	
General expenses	16,600	
Issued share capital: 400,000 €1 shares		400,000

You are given the following additional information on 31/12/2013:
(a) Closing stock €37,500.
(b) Dividend declared 12.5%.

Balance Sheet

1   Match the following terms with the correct explanation.

1	Trading account	**A**	Distribute the net profit as dividends and reserves (retained earnings).
2	Profit and loss account	**B**	Statement of all assets, liabilities and capital of a business on a certain date.
3	Appropriation account	**C**	Calculate the net profit, after all expenses are paid.
4	Balance sheet	**D**	To calculate the working capital of a business.
		E	Calculate the gross profit, difference between sales and cost of sales.

1	2	3	4

2   Explain the following terms.

(a) Balance sheet: _____

_____

(b) Fixed assets: _____

_____

(c) Current assets: _____

_____

3   The following terms appear in either the trading account, the profit and loss account, or the balance sheet of a business. Tick the appropriate box (✔) in each case.

	Trading A/C	Profit and loss A/C	Balance sheet
Vehicles			
Carriage outwards			
Purchases for resale			
Cash			
Debtors			
Customs duty			
Authorised share capital			
Closing stock			
Advertising			

4 Each of the following terms appears in the balance sheet. Identify the appropriate heading for each term by ticking (✔) the correct box.

	Fixed assets	Current assets	Current liabilities	Financed by
Issued share capital				
Creditors				
Closing stock				
Equipment				
Bank				
Premises				
Revenue reserves				
Bank overdraft				
Debtors				

5 List five errors that could affect the trial balance.

(a) _____

(b) _____

(c) _____

(d) _____

(e) _____

6 Explain the following terms.

(a) Authorised share capital: _____

_____

(b) Working capital: _____

_____

(c) Issued share capital: _____

_____

7 Calculate the working capital in each of the following.

(a)	€	(b)	€
Current assets	= 140,000	Current assets	= 476,800
Current liabilities	= 65,000	Current liabilities	= 282,500
Working capital		Working capital	

8 Calculate the total of the current assets in each of the following cases.
(a) Cash €1,200; Bank €9,750; Advertising €3,500; Closing stock €11,650.

(b) Stock (1/1/2013) €14,220; Bank €21,780; Cash €2,100; Stock (31/12/2013) €16,670.

(c) Debtors €6,800; Cash €3,240; Bank overdraft €14,500; Stock (31/12/2013) €22,560.

9 Complete the following balance sheet.

Balance Sheet of Remould Ltd as at 31/12/2013

	€	€	€
Fixed assets			
Premises			460,000
Vehicles			60,000
Current assets			
Stock (31/12/2013)	22,000		
Bank	16,700		
Cash	1,800		
Current liabilities			
Creditors		20,500	
Working capital			
Total net assets			
Financed by			
Authorised share capital	750,000		
Issued share capital:			
400,000 ordinary shares @ €1 each	400,000		
Revenue reserve	65,000	465,000	
Long term liability			
10 year bank loan		75,000	
Capital employed			

10 Tick (✔) the correct answer.
The purchase of equipment by means of a bank term loan affects the balance sheet in which of the following ways:
- Current assets increase and current liabilities decrease. ☐
- Fixed assets increase and current liabilities increase. ☐
- Fixed assets increase and financed by increases. ☐
- Current assets increase and financed by increases. ☐

11 Complete the following balance sheet.

Balance Sheet as at 31/12/2013

	€	€	€
Fixed assets			
Premises			370,000
Equipment			42,000
Vehicles			55,000
Current assets			
Stock (31/12/2013)	19,500		
Debtors	12,800		
Cash	2,700		
Current liabilities			
Bank overdraft		12,000	
Working capital			
Total net assets			
Financed by			
Authorised share capital	500,000		
Issued share capital:			
350,000 ordinary shares @ €1 each	350,000		
Revenue reserve	82,000		
Long term liability			
10 year bank loan		58,000	
Capital employed			

12 Complete the balance sheet from the following information as at 31/12/2013.
Cash €3,000; Bank overdraft €15,000; Premises €265,500; Machinery €87,000; Reserves €60,000; Stock (31/12/2013) €37,500; Authorised share capital €500,000; Issued share capital €300,000; Term loan €18,000.

Balance Sheet as at 31/12/2013

	€	€	€
Fixed assets			
Premises			
Machinery			
Current assets			
Stock (31/12/2013)			
Cash			
Current liabilities			
Bank overdraft			
Working capital			
Total net assets			
Financed by			
Authorised share capital			
Issued share capital:			
300,000 ordinary shares @ €1 each			
Revenue reserve			
Long term liability			
Term loan			
Capital employed			

13 Draft a balance sheet from the following information as at 31/12/2013.
Premises €416,000; Cash €1,200; Equipment €64,000; Vehicles €33,600; Stock (31/12/2013) €13,600; Authorised share capital €600,000; Issued share capital €480,000; Bank overdraft €4,800; Reserves €43,600.

14 Draft a balance sheet from the following information as at 31/12/2013.
Cash €1,950; Machinery €126,000; Bank overdraft €16,200; Delivery van €54,000; Stock (31/12/2013) €37,500; Authorised share capital €750,000; Issued share capital €500,000; Revenue reserve €188,250; Premises €560,000; Long term loan €75,000.

15 Draft a balance sheet from the following information as at 31/12/2013.
Machinery €82,000; Bank €56,000; Cash €6,000; Delivery vans €71,000; Authorised share capital €1,000,000; Stock (31/12/2013) €26,200; Issued share capital €750,000; Reserves €106,500; Furniture & fittings €48,000; Creditors €21,200; Premises €720,000; Long term loan €131,500.

16 Draft a balance sheet from the following information as at 31/12/2013.
Cash €3,600; Bank €23,200; Premises €710,000; Plant & machinery €304,000; Reserves €132,400; Stock (31/12/2013) €30,400; Authorised share capital (€1 shares) €1,000,000; Furniture €50,000; Issued share capital €900,000; Dividend due €48,800; Long term loan €40,000.

17 From the following trial balance, taken from the books of Kramer Ltd as at 31 December 2013, prepare a trading account, profit and loss and appropriation accounts, and the balance sheet at that date. Authorised share capital €400,000. Closing stock at 31/12/2013 is €18,000.

	Dr €	Cr €
Cash sales		371,240
Carriage inwards	16,000	
Cash purchases for resale	249,400	
Opening stock (1/1/2013)	13,680	
Advertising	14,200	
Telephone	4,000	
Salaries and wages	45,600	
Insurance	6,200	
Heating & lighting	8,200	
Dividend paid	14,000	
Bank	21,360	
Cash	600	
Issued share capital in €1 shares		280,000
Premises	280,000	
Furniture & fittings	34,000	
Vehicles	48,000	
Long term loan		104,000
	755,240	755,240

(a) State one reason why a company prepares a trading account each year.

_____

_____

_____

(b) Explain 'dividend paid'. _____

_____

_____

18 From the following trial balance, taken from the books of Alloy Products Ltd as at 31 December 2014, prepare a trading account, profit and loss and appropriation accounts, and the balance sheet at that date. Authorised share capital €600,000. Closing stock at 31/12/2014 is €17,200.

	Dr €	Cr €
Cash sales		545,000
Telephone & Internet	6,200	
Cash purchases for resale	302,000	
Sales & purchases returns	10,000	7,000
Opening stock (1/1/2014)	14,600	
Rent & rates	52,000	
Customs duty	30,200	
Wages	64,000	
Rent received		15,600
Heat & light	7,800	
Dividend paid	32,000	
Equipment	14,400	
Bank overdraft		7,200
Cash	1,600	
Issued share capital in €1 shares		400,000
Premises	364,000	
Vehicles	76,000	
	974,800	974,800

Explain the term 'rent received': _____

_____

19 From the following trial balance, taken from the books of Roches Ltd as at 31 December 2014, prepare a trading account, profit and loss and appropriation accounts, and the balance sheet at that date. Authorised share capital (€1 ordinary shares) €1,000,000. Closing stock at 31/12/2014 is €62,000.

	Dr €	Cr €
Issued capital (€1 shares)		600,000
Cash sales		960,000
Cash purchases for resale	624,000	
Stock (1/1/2014)	44,000	
Carriage inwards	9,000	
Dividend paid	50,000	
Insurance	26,300	
Wages & salaries	109,000	
Interest on bank overdraft	1,700	
Light & heating	20,600	
Telephones	2,400	
Bank overdraft		36,000
Cash	19,000	
Premises	440,000	
Machinery	170,000	
Vehicles	80,000	
	1,596,000	1,596,000

What percentage (%) of sales is the gross profit? _____

20 From the following trial balance, taken from the books of Apex Printers Ltd as at 31 December 2013, prepare a trading account, profit and loss and appropriation accounts, and the balance sheet at that date. Authorised share capital €500,000. Closing stock at 31/12/2013 is €30,000.

	Dr €	Cr €
Cash purchases for resale	385,000	
Cash sales		650,000
Sales & purchases returns	10,000	5,000
Carriage inwards	6,000	
Opening stock (1/1/2013)	28,000	
Cash	4,000	
Dividend paid	20,000	
Heat & light	26,000	
Equipment & fittings	212,000	
Interest on overdraft	900	
Wages	91,000	
Discount received		2,000
Insurance	45,000	
Telephone & Internet	6,100	
Rent & rates	36,000	
Issued share capital		200,000
Bank overdraft		13,000
	870,000	870,000

What does 'dividend paid €20,000' mean? _____

_____

21 From the following trial balance, taken from the books of Kildimo Ltd as at 31 December 2013, prepare a trading account, profit and loss and appropriation accounts, and the balance sheet at that date. Authorised share capital (€1 ordinary shares) €750,000. Closing stock at 31/12/2013 is €42,000.

	Dr €	Cr €
Cash sales		896,000
Cash purchases for resale	532,000	
Customs duty	8,400	
Opening stock (1/1/2013)	39,200	
Wages & salaries	119,000	
Dividend paid	33,600	
Discount received		5,600
Heat & light	36,400	
Equipment & machinery	296,800	
Postage & stationery	9,800	
Rent & rates	56,000	
Cash	5,800	
Advertising	63,000	
Issued share capital		280,000
Bank overdraft		18,400
	1,200,000	1,200,000

Explain the following terms.

(a) Bank overdraft: _____

_____

(b) Appropriation account: _____

_____

22 From the following trial balance, taken from the books of Magus Ltd as at 31 December 2013, prepare a trading account, profit and loss and appropriation accounts, and the balance sheet at that date. Authorised share capital €1,000,000. Closing stock at 31/12/2013 is €52,800.

	Dr €	Cr €
Cash purchases for resale	390,000	
Cash sales		828,000
Sales & purchases returns	17,400	6,000
Cash	1,440	
Opening stock (1/1/2013)	33,600	
Carriage inwards	5,280	
Dividend paid	36,000	
Heat & light	7,560	
Issued share capital		480,000
Interest on overdraft	540	
Wages	144,800	
Rent received		47,200
Insurance	11,400	
Telephone & Internet	6,480	
Premises	548,000	
Bank overdraft		16,120
Machinery & equipment	174,820	
	1,377,320	1,377,320

Give two reasons why limited companies should keep accounts.

(a) _____

(b) _____

Adjustments to the Final Accounts

1 Tick (✔) the correct box.
Rent prepaid is an example of a:
(a) Current asset ☐
(b) Current liability ☐
(c) Unusual gain ☐
(d) Expense ☐

2 Tick (✔) the correct box.
Wages due is an example of a:
(a) Current asset ☐
(b) Current liability ☐
(c) Unusual gain ☐
(d) Fixed asset ☐

3 Tick (✔) the correct box.
Machinery = €60,000. Depreciation @ 15%. The amount of depreciation is:
(a) €15,000 ☐
(b) €9,000 ☐
(c) €51,000 ☐
(d) €69,000 ☐

4 Tick (✔) the correct box.
Vehicles = €90,000. Depreciation @ 20%. The amount of depreciation is:
(a) €108,000 ☐
(b) €72,000 ☐
(c) €18,000 ☐
(d) €20,000 ☐

5 Explain the following terms.

(a) Depreciation: _____

_____

(b) Bad debts: _____

_____

(c) Accrual: _____

_____

6 Calculate the amount prepaid on each of the following (trading period ending 31/12/2013).
(a) Paid annual insurance €8,600 on 1/7/2013.
(b) Paid annual motor tax bill €2,700 on 1/9/2013.
Show the relevant ledger accounts for each, and the extracts from the final accounts.

7 Record the following prepayment in the relevant ledger accounts, for year ended 31/12/2013, showing the balance carried forward, and show the relevant extract from the final accounts: paid annual business insurance of €7,200 on 1/10/2013 by cheque.

8 Record the following prepayment in the relevant ledger account, for year ended 31/12/2013, showing the balance carried forward, and show the relevant extract from the final accounts: paid annual rent of €48,000 on 1/4/2013 by cheque.

9 The following account appeared in the ledger of Regan Products Ltd.

Dr   **Advertising Account**   **Cr**

Date	Details	F	Total	Date	Details	F	Total
31/12	Bank	CB	32,000	31/12	Profit & loss		38,000
31/12	**Balance**	**c/d**	**6,000**				
			38,000				38,000
				1/1/14	**Balance**	**b/d**	**6,000**

What does the balance in this account mean?

_____

_____

_____

10 Record the following accrual in the relevant ledger account, for year ended 31/12/2013, showing the balance carried forward, and show the relevant extract from the final accounts: rent paid (by cheque) for the year €35,000. However, on 31/12/2013, €4,000 in rent is still due.

11 Record the following accrual in the relevant ledger account, for year ended 31/12/2013, showing the balance carried forward, and show the relevant extract from the final accounts: wages paid (by cheque) for the year €165,000. However, on 31/12/2013, €6,000 in wages is still due.

12 Record the following prepayment in the relevant ledger account, for year ended 31/12/2013, showing the balance carried forward, and show the relevant extract from the final accounts: paid the annual advertising bill of €27,000 by cheque on 1 September 2013.

13 Tick (✔) the correct answer.
A firm's profit and loss account showed a net profit of €143,200. The firm's accountant discovered that depreciation €21,500 and commission received €4,300 had been omitted. What was the correct net profit?
(a) €169,000 ☐   **(c)** €117,400 ☐
(b) €126,000 ☐   **(d)** €160,400 ☐

14 Tick (✔) the correct answer.
A firm's profit and loss account showed a net profit of €208,000. The firm's accountant discovered that depreciation €18,400, rent received €10,800, and bad debts €24,000 had been omitted. What was the correct net profit?
(a) €176,400 ☐   **(c)** €239,600 ☐
(b) €261,200 ☐   **(d)** €154,800 ☐

15 Calculate the annual depreciation (straight line) on the following: machinery bought for €65,000, with an expected life of 5 years (no trade-in value). Show the relevant ledger accounts, and the relevant entries in the final accounts.

16 Calculate the annual depreciation (straight line) on the following: vehicles bought for €80,000, with a trade-in value at the end of 6 years of €14,000. Show the relevant ledger accounts, and the relevant entries in the final accounts.

17 Calculate the annual depreciation (straight line) on the following: computer equipment bought for €24,000, with an expected life of 4 years (no trade-in value). Show the relevant ledger accounts, and the relevant entries in the final accounts.

18 On 1 January 2013, Roxboro Ltd purchased office furniture by cheque for €12,000 from Office Supplies Ltd. Roxboro Ltd estimate that the furniture will have a life of 6 years and no trade-in value. The trading year ends on 31 December.
Record the purchase of the office furniture on 1 January 2013 and the annual straight line depreciation written off in 2013 and 2014 in the relevant accounts.

19 On 1 January 2013, Realty Ltd purchased equipment by cheque for €32,000 from O'Brien's Ltd. Realty Ltd estimate that the equipment will have a life of 4 years and a trade-in value of €12,000. The trading year ends on 31 December.
(a) Record the purchase of the delivery van on 1 January 2013 and the annual straight line depreciation written off in 2013 and 2014 in the relevant accounts.
(b) Show the relevant extract in the balance sheet on 31 December 2014.

20 Calculate the amount of money received by the company in each of the following cases.

Debtor: €12,000 Declared bankrupt Paid 10c in the €1	Debtor: €18,000 Declared bankrupt Paid 40c in the €1	Debtor: €6,400 Declared bankrupt Paid 25c in the €1
Bank: € _____ Bad Debt: € _____	Bank: € _____ Bad Debt: € _____	Bank: € _____ Bad Debt: € _____

21 Record the following in the debtor's ledger, general ledger and the final accounts: a debtor, Primex Ltd, who owes us €48,000 is declared bankrupt and pays 20c in the €1.

22 Record the following in the debtor's ledger, general ledger and the final accounts:
a debtor, Hanrahan Ltd, who owes us €32,000 is declared bankrupt and pays 30c in the €1.

23 From the following trial balance, taken as at 31 December 2013, prepare a trading account, profit and loss and appropriation accounts, and the balance sheet at that date. Authorised share capital €600,000.
You are given the following information:
- Closing stock at 31/12/2013 is €26,000.
- Advertising due €7,000.
- Dividend declared 8%.
- Rent receivable prepaid €4,000.
- Depreciation: premises 2%; machinery 15%.

Trial Balance as on 31/12/2013

	Dr	Cr
	€	€
Purchases & sales	168,000	370,000
Purchases returns		8,000
Import duty	7,200	
Wages	70,000	
Advertising	22,000	
Bad debts	6,400	
Commission receivable		12,000
Rent receivable		32,000
Premises	490,000	
Machinery	120,000	
Debtors & creditors	42,400	20,000
Opening stock (1/1/2013)	36,000	
Bank	26,000	
Long term loan		60,000
Revenue reserves		46,000
Issued share capital (€1 shares)		440,000
	988,000	988,000

24 From the following trial balance, taken from the books of Browne Ltd as at 31 December 2013, prepare a trading account, profit and loss and appropriation accounts, and the balance sheet at that date. Authorised share capital €750,000.

You are given the following information:

- Closing stock at 31/12/2013 is €26,000.
- Insurance prepaid €6,000.
- Depreciation: machinery 6%; vehicles 12%.
- Carriage inwards due €1,200.
- Wages due €16,000.

Trial Balance as on 31/12/2013

	Dr	Cr
	€	€
Issued share capital (€1 shares)		500,000
Purchases & sales	86,000	390,000
Carriage inwards	12,800	
Debtors & creditors	46,000	24,000
Sales returns	10,000	
Opening stock (1/1/2013)	14,000	
Commission received		4,000
Advertising	14,000	
Bank overdraft		8,000
Revenue reserves		22,000
Dividends paid	75,000	
Wages & salaries	48,000	
Cash	2,200	
Machinery	490,000	
Vehicles	132,000	
Insurance	18,000	
	948,000	948,000

25 From the following trial balance, as at 31 December 2013, prepare a trading account, profit and loss and appropriation accounts, and the balance sheet at that date. Authorised share capital €750,000.
You are given the following information:
- Closing stock at 31/12/2013 is €54,000.
- Wages & salaries due €18,000.
- Rent receivable prepaid €600.
- Dividend declared 10%.
- Depreciation: equipment 15%; premises 5%.

Give two methods of how a company might reduce its level of bad debts.

Trial Balance as on 31/12/2013

	Dr	Cr
	€	€
Issued share capital (€1 shares)		450,000
Purchases for resale & cash sales	567,000	870,000
Wages & salaries	90,000	
Debtors & creditors	168,000	135,900
Sales returns & purchases returns	33,000	12,000
Bad debts	7,500	
Opening stock (1/1/2013)	43,200	
Rent receivable		23,400
Insurance	25,500	
Bank overdraft		9,000
Import duty on purchases	13,800	
Bank interest	4,800	
Long term loan		60,000
Equipment	240,000	
Cash	7,500	
Premises	360,000	
	1,560,300	1,560,300

26 From the following trial balance, taken from the books of Mayo Ltd as at 31 December 2013, prepare a trading account, profit and loss and appropriation accounts, and the balance sheet at that date. Authorised share capital €2,000,000.
You are given the following information:
- Closing stock at 31/12/2013 is €76,000.
- Advertising due €6,400.
- Commission receivable due €5,600.
- Dividend declared 8%.
- Carriage inwards prepaid €2,000.
- Depreciation: machinery 12%; vehicles 10%.

Trial Balance as on 31/12/2013

	Dr	Cr
	€	€
Purchases for resale & cash sales	464,000	1,120,000
Purchases returns		24,000
Issued share capital (€1 shares)		1,680,000
Debtors & creditors	76,000	62,800
Bad debts	14,400	
Opening stock (1/1/2013)	64,000	
Commission receivable		12,800
Carriage inwards	10,000	
Cash	31,200	
Long term loan		120,000
Buildings	1,320,000	
Wages & salaries	112,000	
Bank overdraft		24,000
Machinery	600,000	
Vehicles	320,000	
Advertising	32,000	
	3,043,600	3,043,600

27 From the following trial balance, taken from the books of Baxter Ltd as at 31 December 2013, prepare a trading account, profit and loss and appropriation accounts, and the balance sheet at that date. Authorised share capital €1,000,000.

You are given the following information:
- Closing stock at 31/12/2013 is €30,000.
- Insurance prepaid €4,320.
- Depreciation: machinery 12%; vehicles 20%.
- Commission receivable due €5,280.
- Dividend declared 5%.

Give two reasons for sales returns.

Trial Balance as on 31/12/2013

	Dr	Cr
	€	€
Purchases for resale & cash sales	132,000	293,280
Sales returns	24,000	
Vehicles	61,680	
Debtors & creditors	108,000	71,520
Buildings	480,000	
Commission receivable		13,920
Insurance	33,600	
Bank overdraft		16,800
Reserves (P & L balance)		72,000
Advertising	16,320	
Machinery	156,000	
Import duty	10,800	
Wages & salaries	36,000	
Cash	9,120	
Opening stock (1/1/2013)	24,000	
Issued share capital (€1 shares)		624,000
	1,091,520	1,091,520

28 From the following trial balance, taken from the books of Sheba Ltd as at 31 May 2013, prepare a trading account, profit and loss and appropriation accounts, and the balance sheet at that date. Authorised share capital €2,000,000. You are given the following information:

- Closing stock at 31/5/2013 is €77,500.
- Advertising prepaid €4,000.
- Dividend declared 12%.
- Import duty due €2,250.
- Depreciation: plant & equipment 15%; vehicles 20%.

Trial Balance as on 31/5/2013

	Dr	Cr
	€	€
Purchases for resale & cash sales	430,000	970,000
Sales returns & purchases returns	17,500	21,000
Wages	120,000	
Opening stock (1/6/2012)	65,000	
Commission receivable		28,000
Reserves (P & L balance)		80,000
Debtors & creditors	131,500	58,000
Insurance	31,000	
Bank	39,750	
Vehicles	175,000	
Cash	8,500	
Import duty	36,750	
Advertising	82,000	
Plant & equipment	520,000	
Issued share capital (€1 shares)		1,250,000
Premises	750,000	
	2,407,000	2,407,000

29 From the following trial balance, taken from the books of Logan Ltd as at 30 June 2013, prepare a trading account, profit and loss and appropriation accounts, and the balance sheet at that date. Authorised share capital €1,000,000. You are given the following information:

- Closing stock at 30/6/2013 is €32,500.
- Rent receivable prepaid €5,000.
- Dividend declared 8%.
- Insurance due €8,750.
- Depreciation: premises 2%; machinery 15%.

Trial Balance as on 30/6/2013

	Dr	Cr
	€	€
Purchases for resale & cash sales	210,000	462,500
Purchases returns		10,000
Wages & salaries	87,500	
Opening stock (1/7/2012)	45,000	
Rent receivable		55,000
Reserves (P & L balance)		57,500
Cash	2,500	
Insurance	27,500	
Bank	30,000	
Long term loan		75,000
Debtors & creditors	53,000	25,000
Carriage inwards	9,000	
Bad debts	8,000	
Machinery	150,000	
Issued share capital (€1 shares)		550,000
Premises	612,500	
	1,235,000	1,235,000

30 From the following trial balance, taken from the books of Kielys Ltd as at 31 July 2013, prepare a trading account, profit and loss and appropriation accounts, and the balance sheet at that date. Authorised share capital €750,000. You are given the following information:
- Closing stock at 31/7/2013 is €29,500.
- Insurance prepaid €2,250.
- Carriage inwards due €1,500.
- Depreciation: machinery 10%; vehicles 15%.

Calculate the rate of dividend paid to the shareholders of Kielys Ltd.

Trial Balance as on 31/7/2013

	Dr	Cr
	€	€
Debtors & creditors	57,000	43,250
Purchases for resale & cash sales	370,000	775,000
Sales returns & purchases returns	14,000	38,000
Wages	114,500	
Opening stock (1/8/2012)	35,000	
Commission receivable		30,000
Bank interest	15,000	
Machinery	350,000	
Dividends paid	120,000	
Insurance	14,750	
Bank overdraft		19,500
Vehicles	275,000	
Cash	3,500	
Carriage inwards	22,000	
Rent & rates	65,000	
Long term loan		150,000
Issued share capital (€1 shares)		400,000
	1,455,750	1,455,750

Reporting on Accounts

1   Explain the term liquidity. _____

_____

_____

Insert the correct ratios.

Current Ratio	Acid-test Ratio

2   Explain the term solvency. _____

_____

_____

Insert the correct formula.

Solvency

3   Explain stock turnover. _____

_____

_____

Insert the correct formula.

Stock turnover

4 Explain the term profitability. _____

_____

_____

Insert the correct formulae.

Gross margin	**Net margin**	**Return on investment**

5 Calculate the (a) current ratio and (b) the acid-test ratio for each of the following.

(a) Current assets = €360,000; current liabilities = €150,000; closing stock = €60,000.
(b) Current assets = €150,000; current liabilities = €75,000; closing stock = €30,000.

6 Calculate the (a) current ratio and (b) the acid-test ratio for each of the following.

(a) Current assets = €216,000; current liabilities = €120,000; closing stock = €108,000.
(b) Current assets = €68,200; current liabilities = €31,000; closing stock = €35,650.

7 Explain three limitations of final accounts and balance sheets in assessing a business.

(a) _____

(b) _____

(c) _____

8 Calculate the stock turnover for the following.
Cost of sales = €645,000
Opening stock = €24,000
Closing stock = €19,000

9 Calculate the stock turnover for the following.
Cost of sales = €297,000
Stock (1/1/2013) = €12,400
Stock (31/12/2013) = €14,600

10 Calculate the stock turnover for the following and comment on the answer.
Cost of sales = €295,200
Opening stock = €26,400
Closing stock = €22,800

11 Calculate the stock turnover for the following and comment on the answer.
Cost of sales = €109,200
Opening stock = €7,100
Closing stock = €8,500

12 Identify the source of the information needed to calculate the following: tick the appropriate boxes (✔).

	Trading account	Profit & loss account	Balance sheet
Stock turnover			
Current ratio			
Acid-test ratio			
Solvency			
Net margin			
Gross margin			
Return on investment			

13 Calculate the (a) gross margin, (b) net margin and (c) return on investment from the following: sales = €720,000; gross profit = €432,000; net profit = €172,800; capital employed = €1,200,000.

14 Calculate the (a) gross margin, (b) net margin and (c) return on investment from the following: sales = €160,000; gross profit = €56,000; net profit = €24,000; capital employed = €300,000.

15 Calculate the (a) gross margin, (b) net margin and (c) return on investment from the following: sales = €840,000; gross profit = €235,200; net profit = €92,400; capital employed = €1,000,000.

16 Calculate the (a) gross margin, (b) net margin and (c) return on investment from the following: sales = €470,000; gross profit = €131,600; net profit = €65,800; capital employed = €800,000.

17 The following figures appeared in a firm's final accounts for the year ending 31 December 2013: gross profit = €408,000; cost of sales = €216,000; net margin = 14%.
Calculate the (a) sales and (b) net profit.

18 The following figures appeared in a firm's final accounts for the year ending 31 December 2013: gross profit = €63,000; cost of sales = €140,000; net margin = 15%; capital employed = €700,000.
Calculate the (a) sales, (b) net profit and (c) return on investment.

19 Calculate the time it takes to pay creditors (in days) from the following information.

(a) Credit purchases = €360,000
   Creditors = €24,658

(b) Credit purchases = €590,000
   Creditors = €42,836

20 Calculate the time it takes debtors to pay the business (in days) from the following information.

(a) Credit sales = €415,000
   Debtors = €36,952

(b) Credit sales = €700,000
   Debtors = €69,041

21

Balance Sheet as at 31 December 2013

	€	€
Fixed assets		485,000
Current assets	180,000	
(incl. closing stock €48,000)		
Current liabilities	120,000	
		60,000
		545,000
Financed by:	Authorised capital	Issued capital
Ordinary shares	500,000	350,000
Revenue reserve		95,000
		445,000
Long term loan		100,000
		545,000

(a) What is the figure for working capital? _____

(b) What is the figure for retained earnings (revenue reserve)? _____

(c) Calculate the current ratio and the acid-test ratio. _____

_____

_____

(d) If the net profit was €35,425, calculate the return on investment. _____

_____

_____

22

Balance Sheet as at 31/12/2013

	€	€
Fixed assets		685,000
Current assets	288,000	
(incl. closing stock €64,000)		
Current liabilities	160,000	128,000
		813,000
Financed by:		
Authorised capital €750,000		
Issued capital ordinary shares	500,000	
Revenue reserve	163,000	
		663,000
Term loan		150,000
		813,000

(a) What is the figure for working capital? _____

(b) What is the figure for retained earnings (revenue reserve)? _____

(c) Calculate the current ratio and the acid-test ratio. _____

_____

_____

(d) If the net profit was €65,040 calculate the return on investment. _____

_____

_____

23 Examine the final accounts and balance sheets of O'Mara Ltd for the years 2013 and 2014. Compare and comment on the performance of the company for the two years using the following ratios (show workings):
(a) Gross margin.   **(b)** Net margin.   **(c)** Return on capital employed.
(d) Acid-test (quick) ratio.   **(e)** Rate of dividend paid.

2013 Trading, Profit and Loss and Appropriation Account for the year ended 31/12/2013		2014 Trading, Profit and Loss and Appropriation Account for the year ended 31/12/2014	
Sales	608,000	Sales	736,000
Gross profit	240,000	Gross profit	262,400
Net profit	137,600	Net profit	176,000
Dividends paid	45,760	Dividends paid	54,080
Reserves	91,840	Reserves	121,920

Balance Sheet as at 31/12/2013	€	€	Balance Sheet as at 31/12/2014	€	€
Fixed assets		576,000	Fixed assets		633,600
Current assets (including closing stock 22,400)	82,240		Current assets (including closing stock 22,400)	117,760	
Less current liabilities	54,400	27,840	Less current liabilities	57,600	60,160
		603,840			693,760
Financed by 416,000 €1 ordinary shares (issued)		416,000	Financed by 416,000 €1 ordinary shares (issued)		416,000
Reserves		91,840	Reserves		213,760
Long term liabilities		96,000	Long term liabilities		64,000
		603,840			693,760

24 Examine the final accounts and balance sheets of Poca Ltd for the years 2013 and 2014. Compare and comment on the performance of the company for the two years using ratios (show workings):
(a) Gross margin.   (b) Net margin.   (c) Return on capital employed.
(d) Acid-test (quick) ratio.   (e) Rate of dividend paid.

2013 Trading, Profit and Loss and Appropriation Account for the year ended 31/12/2013		2014 Trading, Profit and Loss and Appropriation Account for the year ended 31/12/2014	
Sales	900,000	Sales	1,235,000
Gross profit	630,000	Gross profit	741,000
Net profit	234,000	Net profit	247,000
Dividends paid	63,700	Dividends paid	68,250
Reserves	170,300	Reserves	178,750

Balance Sheet as at 31/12/2013

	€	€
Fixed assets		1,079,000
Current assets (including closing stock 26,000)	189,800	
Less current liabilities	84,500	105,300
		1,184,300
Financed by		
910,000 €1 ordinary shares (issued)		910,000
Reserves		170,300
Long term liabilities		104,000
		1,184,300

Balance Sheet as at 31/12/2014

	€	€
Fixed assets		1,066,000
Current assets (including closing stock 24,700)	351,650	
Less current liabilities	54,600	297,050
		1,363,050
Financed by		
910,000 €1 ordinary shares		910,000
Reserves		349,050
Long term liabilities		104,000
		1,363,050

Complete the report on today's date, to the Board of Directors, based on the results of your findings and commenting on any trends.

25 Explain the following terms.

(a) Issued share capital: _____

_____

(b) Solvency: _____

_____

(c) Overtrading: _____

_____

26 James Ltd has the following results for year ending 31/12/2013.

Rate of stock turnover	8 times
Net profit percentage	16%
Acid-test ratio	2.5 : 1
Return on capital employed	7%

James Ltd supply the following information for the year ending 31/12/2014.

Net sales	€306,000	Net profit	€36,720
Opening stock	€21,000	Current assets (incl. closing stock)	€225,100
Closing stock	€25,000	Current liabilities	€87,000
Cost of sales	€161,000	Capital employed	€612,000

Calculate the following ratios for **2014**.

(a) Rate of stock turnover.

(b) Acid-test ratio.

(c) Net profit percentage.

(d) Return on capital employed.

Compare 2013 and 2014 and comment on any trends in the form of a report on today's date.

27 Mathews Ltd has the following results for year ending 31/12/2013.

Rate of stock turnover	6 times
Rate of dividend	12%
Current ratio	2 : 1
Return on capital employed	15%

Mathews Ltd supply the following information for the year ending 31/12/2014.

Average stock	€42,000	Net profit	€112,800
Issued share capital	€720,000	Current assets (incl. closing stock)	€108,000
Dividend paid	€57,600	Current liabilities	€72,000
Cost of sales	€210,000	Capital employed	€940,000

Calculate the following ratios for **2014**.

(a) Rate of stock turnover.

(b) Current ratio.

(c) Rate of dividend.

(d) Return on capital employed.

Compare 2013 and 2014 and comment on any trends in the form of a report on today's date.

Service Firms

Exercises Based on Chapter Content

1 Complete the following sentences.
The usual accounts kept by a service firm are:

(a) _____ cash book (cash _____ and cheque payments).

(b) _____ operating statement.

(c) A balance _____ is then prepared.

2 List the source documents for an analysed cash book. _____

_____

_____

3 Tick the boxes (✔) to indicate **true** or **false**.

	True	False
(a) Revenue commissioners are also known as the tax office.		
(b) Accounts are not needed to apply for a bank loan.		
(c) Purchase of fixed assets is shown in the operating statement.		
(d) Drawings is when the owner puts money into the business.		
(e) The balance at the beginning of the analysed cash is the closing cash of the business.		
(f) Service firms produce a product.		

4 Total and balance the following account.

Analysed Cash Book of Streetcar Taxis for One Week

Date	Details	Total	Fares	Deliveries	School	Date	Details	Total	Petrol	Wages	Repairs
Oct						Oct					
2	School	180			180	3	M. Adams	257		257	
4	Passengers	280	280			5	Topaz Oil	80	80		
7	Parcels	277		277		7	J. Jaffer	320		320	
8	Passengers	490	490			8	OK Garage	50			50
9	Parcel	420		420		10	M. Adams	290		290	
11	School	110			110	12	Topaz Oil	120	120		
14	School	125			125	14	OK Garage	160			160
						15	OK Garage	180	180		
							Balance				
	Balance										

5 Complete the following operating statement.

Income	€	€
Receipts from taxi customers		77,000
Deliveries		35,500
School collections		12,000
Less expenses		
Petrol	6,500	
Wages	20,000	
Repairs to cars	16,500	
Insurance	8,000	
Advertising	2,500	
Telephone	1,400	
Electricity	2,200	
Rent	12,000	
Cleaning	1,400	
Bank charges	900	
Profit		

Farm Accounts

Exercises Based on Chapter Content

1   What is a dairy farm? _____

What is a tillage farm? _____

2   List three problems faced by all farmers.

(a) _____

(b) _____

(c) _____

3   What is the SFP? _____

What is a herd number? _____

4   List some of the source documents for farm accounts. _____

_____

_____

5   Total the analysis columns and balance the following analysed cash book.

Date April	Details	Total	Milk	Calves	Other	Date April	Details	Total	Electricity	Feed	Repairs	Vet	Other
2	Dairy co-op	6,700	6,700			3	Diesel	600					600
7	Mart	4,000		4,000		4	Feed Ltd	1,200		1,200			
16	SFP	1,200			1,200	5	Medicine	300				300	
						8	ESB	560	560				
						10	Feed Ltd	500		500			
						14	Repairs	400			400		
						16	Fencing	130					130
						19	Cleaners	246					246
						22	Parts	220			220		
						25	Vet	50				50	
						26	Feed	300		300			
							Balance						
	Balance												

6 Tick the appropriate box (✔) to indicate if the following are revenue or capital expenditure for a farmer.

	Capital expenditure	Revenue expenditure
Purchase of new tractor.		
Road tax for new tractor.		
Repairs to feed bin.		
Electricity bill.		
Purchase of land.		
Mobile phone top up.		
Purchase of 10 sheep.		
Paid for 2 tonnes of cattle feed.		
Repair to roof of dairy.		
Extension to concrete yard.		
Rewiring of milking shed.		
New lock for animal medicine press.		
Replacement of worn out tyre for cattle trailer.		
Fertiliser for land.		

7 Fill in the blanks using the information for Martin Caora on page 418 of the textbook.

What is the total income for M. Caora on 31 December 2011? _____

What is the net profit _____. Total fixed assets _____

Working capital _____. Capital employed _____

What would be the effect on the accounts if an additional vet bill for €900 which was omitted when the

accounts were drafted is now included on net profit? _____

_____

8 List three reasons why farmers should keep accounts.

(a) _____

(b) _____

(c) _____

9   Examine the accounts of James Nash on page 419 of the textbook and answer the following questions.

(a) Name his accountants. _____

(b) What rate of depreciation is applied to machinery each year? _____

(c) What is the gross profit? _____

    Net profit? _____. Total fixed assets? _____

(d) Calculate the following ratios.

    (i) Current ratio: _____

    (ii) Acid-test: _____

    (iii) Return on capital employed: _____

(e) Calculate the net profit if the following changes occur: single farm payment reduced by 8%, sales drop by 40%, diesel drops by 5% and labour drops by 20%. _____

(f) Recalculate the return on investment ratio in the light of the changes in (e). _____

Club Accounts

Exercises Based on Chapter Content

1   What is the aim of a business? _____

2   What is the aim of a tennis club? _____

      What is the aim of a golf club? _____

3   Name three club officers. _____

4   List four items that may appear on a club agenda for an AGM.

      (a) _____

      (b) _____

      (c) _____

      (d) _____

5   Fill in the blanks in the following chart of club officers and their functions.

Club officers	Functions
Chairperson	• Organise _____ with the secretary. • Overall running of club. • Carry out _____ taken at the club meetings. • Chair club meetings.
	• Inform members of meetings. • Report to the AGM. • Record the discussions and decisions of meetings (minutes).
	• Promotes the club to the public, e.g. newspapers, radio etc.
Treasurer	• Responsible for the club's _____. • Must account for all money received and spent. • Collecting membership fees (_____).

6   Fill in the blanks in the following chart.

Club records	Company records
	Cash book
	Profit and loss account
	Profit
	Loss
	Capital

7 List four functions of the club treasurer.

(a) _____

(b) _____

(c) _____

(d) _____

8 Balance the following analysed cash book.

Dr   Analysed Cash Book for Teenzone Youth Club   **Cr**

Date 2013	Details	Total (€)	Members' subs	Jukebox	Disco	Date	Details	Total (€)	Jukebox	Disco	Repairs & renewals
1 Sept						Sept					
	Balance	400				3	Rent (jukebox)	140	140		
6	Membership	160	160			5	New lock	20			20
12	CDs	28		28		8	Jukebox	60	60		
16	Tickets	36			36	10	Posters	40		40	
18	CDs	32		32		12	Repairs to jukebox	76	76		
20	Tickets	32			32	19	Fee DJ 1	40		40	
22	Tickets	380			380	22	Fee DJ 2	52		52	
23	Membership	450	450			31	Balance				
1 Oct	Balance										

9 Calculate the accumulated fund for the following.

Assets		Liabilities		Accumulated fund
(a) Premises	€70,000	Bank overdraft	€23,000	
Equipment	€23,000			
Cash	€899			
(b) Tennis courts	€56,000	Excess income	€56,000	
Clubhouse	€100,000			
Cash	€700			
(c) Playing fields	€78,000	Bank overdraft	€2,000	
Minibus	€20,000			
Cash	€12,000			

10 Examine the report from Tim Walsh, Treasurer to the Ballygrennan Historical Society on page 429 of the textbook and answer the following questions.

(a) How much cash in hand has the Society got? _____

(b) Who do they bank with? _____

(c) What is the highest expense of the club? _____

Higher Level Questions

11 Calculate the revised bar profit of Allagaun Gaels GAA Club (see page 430 of the textbook) if the following changes apply: opening stock increase by €500 and depreciate fixtures by 15%.

12 Calculate the revised excess income and re-do the balance sheet for Allagaun Gaels GAA Club (see page 431 of the textbook).

Fixed assets	€	€	€
Playing fields			
Clubhouse			
Training lanes/dressing rooms			
Fixtures and fittings			
Field equipment			
Bar equipment			
Current assets			
Bar stock			
Insurance prepaid			
Cash			
Stock/hurleys			
Team jerseys			
Current liabilities			
ESB due			
Bank overdraft			
Working capital			
Total assets			
Financed by			
Accumulated fund			
Excess income			

13 Look at the final accounts of Allagaun Gaels GAA Club (see page 431 of the textbook) and calculate the following.

(a) The new figure for subscriptions if the 3% increase is employed. _____

(b) Bar profit if bar sales dropped by 12%. _____

Practice Paper 1 for Ordinary Level

Section A (100 marks)

Answer all 20 questions. Each question carries 5 marks.

1 Explain the following terms.

(a) ATM: _____

(b) PAYE: _____

(c) PRSI: _____

2 Place the following names in alphabetical order.
Niall Collins; Nora Corbett; Pat Coman.

_____

3 Mary is paid €9 per hour. She worked 39 hours last week. Calculate her gross pay.

_____

Mary worked 2 hours overtime at double time. How much extra will she receive in her gross pay?

_____

4 Name the currencies of the following countries.

(a) France: _____

(b) Spain; _____

(c) America: _____

5 Nathan has €15 to spend. His choices are cinema tickets for two people, a new DVD or flowers for Mother's Day. He picks the DVD. What is the opportunity cost of the DVD?

_____

6 In a family budget, spending on rent is considered to be _____ expenditure.

7 Balance the following account.

Date		Total €	Date		Total €
	Cash	100		Clothes	56
	Lotto win	15		Shopping	45

8 Tick the boxes (✔) to indicate **true** or **false**.

	True	False
(a) Expenditure is money received.		
(b) The government pays the wages of Gardaí and teachers.		

9 If government expenditure is bigger than government spending, it has a _____ budget.

10 What is a bar code? _____

_____

11 Give one example of a valid complaint. _____

_____

12 Cornflakes may be bought in two sizes: small 250 grams €4 and large 500 grams €7. Which is better value?

_____

13 Give one example of a brand name. _____

14 Name three methods of written communication.

(a) _____

(b) _____

(c) _____

15 Hardware for a computer is _____

_____

16 List three uses of computers and technology in a supermarket.

(a) _____

(b) _____

(c) _____

17 What do the initials www stand for? _____

18 What is the difference between work and employment? _____

_____

19 List three rights of an employee.

(a) _____

(b) _____

(c) _____

20 Give one example of a trade union. _____

Section B (300 marks)

Answer all 5 questions. Each question carries 60 marks.

1 Draft the household budget for the White family for the months of June, July, August and September.
- Opening cash €1,700.
- Noel White earns €1,200 monthly and expects a bonus in June of €400.
- Nora White earns €1,300 monthly.
- They receive child benefit of €120 per month.
- The mortgage payments are €670 per month.
- Electricity costs are €120 in June and €80 in August.
- They have a land line and broadband costing €145 per month.
- Car running costs are €120 per month with a reduction of €60 in August.
- Car insurance costs €400 in July and car tax is €123 in August.
- Entertainment costs €230 monthly, rising to €350 in August only.
- The family expects to pay €2,000 for a holiday in August.
- Their wedding anniversary will cost €200 in September.

	June	July	Aug	Sept	Total
Salary Noel White					
Salary Nora White					
Child benefit					
Total					
Fixed					
Mortgage					
Telephone					
Subtotal					
Irregular					
Electricity					
Car running costs					
Car insurance					
Subtotal					
Discretionary					
Entertainment					
Holiday					
Wedding anniversary					
Subtotal					
Total expenditure					
Net cash					
Opening cash					
Closing cash					

2 Jerry McCarthy of 23 Coolgreen, Ballyfehane, Cork, purchased a set of alloy wheels for his car from HiValue Motor Factors, 89 Sean Flynn Road, Blackrock, Cork on 21 May 2011. He paid €450 cash and received a receipt from the shop assistant.

He paid Quality Motors of Coolgreen, Ballyfehane, Cork, to fit the wheels on 23 May 2011. They informed him that two of the alloy wheels did not match and were not the correct size for his car.

He wrote to HiValue Motor Factors on the same day complaining about the alloys, looking for replacement for the two wheels and gave his contact details. His telephone number is 086 9876543.

(a) Write the letter that Jerry sent on 23 May 2011.

(b) List the rights that Jerry has under the Sale of Goods and Supply of Services Act.

(c) Name an organisation that Jerry could complain to if he does not get a good response to his letter.

(d) Name a magazine published by a consumer organisation.

3 Your neighbour wishes to buy a personal computer (PC) for his son who is going to the Institute of Technology in September. He wishes to use it for the Internet, word processing, booking flights, CAD and spreadsheet.

The following advertisement appeared in the local newspaper.

Bacer PC for sale

5MG memory, webcam, DVD, wireless mouse.
€700 or 50 payments of €18.
Contact: The Manager, Computer Country,
Belan Industrial Estate, Limerick

(a) Explain the following terms.

(i) 5MG memory: _____

(ii) Webcam: _____

(iii) DVD: _____

(iv) Wireless mouse: _____

(b) List three other input devices that a computer may have.

(i) _____

(ii) _____

(iii) _____

(c) Work out the payments for the computer and comment on them. _____

_____

_____

(d) Explain the following terms.

   (i) Internet: _____

   (ii) Word processing: _____

   (iii) Booking flights: _____

   (iv) CAD: _____

   (v) Spreadsheet: _____

(e) As well as a computer and Internet access, what else in needed to book flights on the Internet?

_____

(f) List other uses of a PC. _____

_____

4 Examine this diagram of the consumer rights card.

NAT**I**ONAL CONSUMER AGENCY | **Shoppers' Rights Card**

Remember:
- **Always ask for a receipt.**
- **If you have a complaint, act quickly.**
- **You are not entitled to a refund if you simply change your mind.**

For more info about your consumer rights, visit www.consumerconnect.ie or LoCall 1890 432 432.

Goods (including those bought in a sale) must:
- fit the description given.
- be fit for their purpose.
- be of a quality fit for sale.
- match any sample shown.
- have the full retail price clearly displayed.

If not, the law says the retailer must fix the problem.

You are entitled to:
- have repaired, replaced or refunded, any goods that turn out to be faulty or wrongly described.
- go to the Small Claims Court if you are not happy with the retailer's response.

(a) What does the law state about goods bought (even in a sale)? _____

_____

(b) Who must fix any problem that occurs with an item purchased? _____

_____

(c) What is a consumer who has purchased faulty goods entitled to? _____

_____

(d) Write an informative note on the Small Claims Court. _____

_____

_____

(e) What advice does the National Consumer Agency give to consumers? _____

_____

_____

(f) What is the website for the National Consumer Agency? _____

(g) What is the telephone number for the National Consumer Agency? _____

5 You purchased a hairdryer from Pizza Electrical, 23 Main Street, Portarlington, Co. Laois on Saturday 20 December 2011. When you used it for the first time it would not heat up properly and indeed got cooler when used for a long time. Your hair did not look well and you are very disappointed with the result.
You wrote to Pizza Electrical on 3 January 2012 and complained about the product. You explained that the hairdryer was not fit for its purpose and asked for a refund. You wrote that you would bring the hairdryer into the shop on the following Saturday at 3pm. A copy of the receipt is attached to the letter.

(a) Write the letter to Pizza Electrical using your own address.